This Was a Man
Authorized Biography of
Boxing Champion Joey Giardello

This Was a Man
Authorized Biography of
Boxing Champion Joey Giardello

By Charles Redner

The true story of boxing middleweight champion Joey
Giardello, once anointed the "Bad Boy of Boxing," and his
wife, Rosalie, who redirected their lives for the benefit of
their son, Carman, born with Down syndrome.

Introduction by Vince Papale

PUBLISHING

This Was a Man
Authorized Biography of
Boxing Champion Joey Giardello

Printed in the United States of America

Ri Publishing
Laguna Woods, CA 92637

charles@charlesredner.com
www. charlesredner.com

Republish of *Down But Never Out*, 2010

ISBN: 978-0-9855583-5-2

Dedication

For Robert H. Adleman, author of *The Devil's Brigade* and eight other books. More than my first employer, he doubled as a mentor who opened my eyes to a world that I had not known existed before he revealed it. He paved the way for my career in advertising, broadcasting, publishing and writing where all things became possible. This book reflects it.

*"What You Leave Behind Is Not
What Is Engraved In Stone Monuments,
But What Is Woven Into The Lives Of Others."*

—Pericles

CONTENTS

An 18-year-old Giardello poses for a publicity photo. After a few bouts, a quick-handed opponent never saw an opening like this during a fight.

Introduction

Will the real Rocky please stand up?

By Vince Papale

The once-popular television game show, *To Tell the Truth,* always ended with the master of ceremonies asking one of three guests to rise when asked, "Will the real (fill in the name) please stand up?" I was thinking, what if? What would have happened if Sylvester Stallone, Vince Papale, and Joey Giardello were seated and the host queried, "Will the real Rocky please stand up?" Who would have stood? I imagined that all of us would have risen, but two would eventually have to sit down.

One of the two would have surprised the gathering.

Yes, Stallone wrote and starred in the 1976 blockbuster movie and its sequels, but his Rocky was a fictional character. He would sit down. Meanwhile, with my rise from the projects to a thirty-year-old professional football player with the Philadelphia

Eagles, many would say that I could have qualified for the Rocky nickname. Jim Murray, the Eagles' general manager at the time, proffered the idea of promoting me as a real-life Rocky immediately after the film's release and phenomenal success. My agent even printed tee-shirts with a picture of me that were captioned: "Philly's Own Rocky."

As inspirational as my story might be, Rocky was, of course, a boxer. I was not. So I'd be next to sit.

That would leave only Joey Giardello standing. And rightly so! The former middleweight champion lived as close to the Rocky theme as anyone ever did before or after the film created the fictional legend.

The rise of Carmine Tilelli (who took the name Joey Giardello so he could join the paratroopers without parental approval) from a modest upbringing to a Boxing Hall of Fame middleweight champion classifies him, to me, as the best choice for a real-life Rocky. He knew and socialized with celebrities from the worlds of entertainment, politics, sports, and business, including Vice President Richard Nixon, President John F. Kennedy, Senator Edward F. Kennedy, Frank Sinatra, and Joe DiMaggio. Duke Snider, Peewee Reese, Carl Furillo, and the rest of his beloved 1950s-era Brooklyn Dodgers were all friends. So was another Dodger with powerful Philly ties, former L.A. manager Tommy Lasorda. Giardello, of course, rooted for the Phillies when he moved to the City of Brotherly Love.

I first met Joey when he was a member of a football "chain gang" while I played for a World Football League team. I saw him on the sidelines and was in total awe. While in uniform, I wanted to shake the hand of a legend. The rest of the story remains untold. I also attended the ceremony when Joey was inducted into the Philadelphia Chapter of the Italian American Sports Hall of Fame.

But there was far more to the man and his legacy than boxing and baseball. Joey was first and foremost a husband, and a father to four boys. His second son, Carman, born with Down syndrome, produced his own Rocky fairy tale. During and after his retirement from boxing, Joey raised thousands of dollars for his two favorite charities, St. John of God School for special needs children and the Special Olympics. He assisted Eunice Shriver when she launched the Special Olympics in 1968. Then in 1970, at the second games, Carman won gold. The image of the former world middleweight champion hugging his gold medal-winning champion son, a kid who really defied the odds, is one of the many moments Charles Redner shares with all of us in *This Was a Man.*

Joey died in September 2008, but his heritage will live on. Within the pages of *This Was a Man,* the true spirit of the man is revealed for all to see. Joey may have been down on occasion, but in the ring, he was never knocked out. The same applied in life. Now experience the dynamism and humanitarianism of Joey Giardello, champion boxer and champion father, and my choice for the "real" Philadelphia Rocky.

Vince Papale #83 Eagles, Cherry Hill, New Jersey,

December 2009

Author's note: The Vince Papale story, told in the book and movie, Invincible *(2006), which starred Mark Wahlberg, provided an imposing platform for Vince to continue his inspirational journey. As a successful teacher, professional football player, and a cancer survivor, Papale has experienced many of the highs and lows life can present, but he always accents the positive. Now he actively encourages others to achieve their life's goals. With the publication of his next book,* Be Invincible! *Papale plans to continue helping others across the country advance their own "Invincible" dreams.*

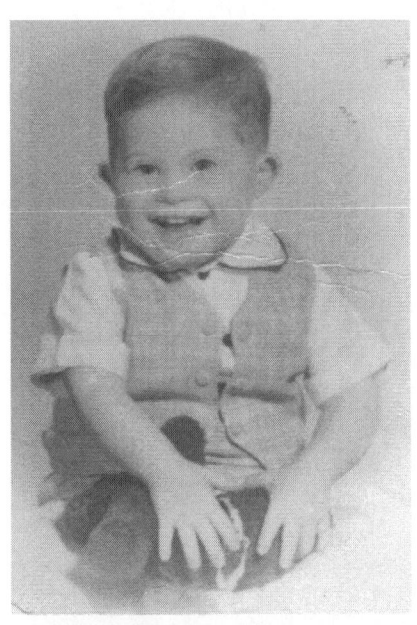

Baby Carman (circa 1955—top) Dad (Joey Giardello) gives son, Carman, a boxing lesson in Cherry Hill home's family room—mantle filled with the champ's trophies, above them world middleweight title belt.

Prologue

The Knockout Birth

February 5, 1954 • Philadelphia, PA

Rosalie Tilelli sat up straight, three pillows stuck between her back and the head of the hospital bed. She cradled her five-day-old son, Carman, in one arm. Her eyes locked onto a tiny black and white television set propped upon a food cart across the room, the portable set with its rabbit ears adjusted for the best possible reception. The grainy, flipping video made for difficult viewing, but Rosalie was delighted that the hospital staff had gone to the trouble for her. "Carman, you have to watch this fight with me. It's your daddy's first since you were born." She gently shook her arm; two green eyes blinked open. The baby wrinkled his nose but didn't cry.

The miniature figures on the screen were standing in the center of a boxing ring. The 10:00 p.m. telecast originated from New York City's Madison Square Garden, the Mecca of boxing. One combatant, her husband, Joey Giardello, smiled cordially at his opponent as the referee addressed the warriors: "*Watch the low blows, no holding behind the head, in case of a knock down go to a neutral corner, break when I say so; let's have a clean fight.*" Rosalie leaned forward to hear the TV commentary, the volume turned down to near inaudible in deference to the late hour.

Two chatting nurses walked into Rosalie's room together; one strode to the end of the bed, removed Rosalie's chart, made a note and placed it back on the hook. The second nurse handed Rosalie a warmed baby bottle and flopped down on the bed. "Is it time?" she asked, looking over at the television.

"The ref's giving instructions. It'll start in a minute," Rosalie replied.

The note-jotting nurse smiled at Rosalie and walked out the room. Rosalie placed the bottle in Carman's tiny mouth, her attention wholly focused on the television. Carman held the nipple in his mouth, lips not moving. Rosalie keyed on the boxing match. "This is Carman's first chance to see his father fight. I want to remember this moment," Rosalie said as she looked over at the nurse.

※ ※ ※

The referee nodded and the boxers hiked back to their corners. Joey hurried faster than usual. He lectured his trainer and cut man standing on the apron just outside the ropes, "Guys. I gotta get out of here. Rosey's still in the hospital with the newborn and I wanna see them tonight." He took a deep breath and held it, puffing up his reddening cheeks. The crowd babble rose in anticipation of the bell.

"We know, Joey," said Joe Pollini, his trainer, "but watch this guy for a few rounds. He could be dangerous early."

"*Nessuna tale fortuna*" (No such luck), responded Joey. Pollini jerked a towel off his fighter's neck as the bell rang.

Joey quickly turned, met his opponent in the center of the ring. Determined to end the fight quickly, he pursued the attack.

Before the fight crowd had completely settled back into their seats for the main event, Joey dropped Walter Cartier on the canvas, not once but twice.

Some boxing writers would suggest that Joey Giardello didn't have a killer's instinct when he had an opponent in trouble, but that wasn't the case—at least on this night. Knowing the three-knockdown rule applied, Joey hastily threw punches from every angle, landing many. A looping right connected. The retreating Cartier stumbled backward. Gravity did the rest. The middleweight tumbled for the third knockdown, giving Giardello the win.

※ ※ ※

Rosalie watched the referee wave her husband away from the fallen Cartier and raise Joey's arm in victory. In less than three minutes of the first round, Joey had notched the win.

"Wow! That was fast! See, Carman? Daddy just won this fight for you," said Rosalie. Even she was surprised by how quickly it had ended.

"Here's Carman." She handed the newborn over to the nurse.

The nurse lifted the baby from Rosalie. Let's go; time for beddy-bye, Carman." She walked over to the television, turned it off, and marched out of the room with the baby.

Years after, Carman would joke that he remembered that fight.

❋ ❋ ❋

Dawn approached as Joey pulled his car across the street from Methodist Hospital in South Philadelphia and parked. He shut off the engine and sat for a moment to revel in his thoughts. He let the radio play. Dean Martin's "That's Amore" blasted from car speakers. Joey loved Dean's music and this song was definitely one of his favorites. He sang along, "When you dance down the street with a cloud at your feet. You're in love." The recording ended; he turned the volume knob down until the radio clicked off. Joey *was* in love—in love with the whole world. Yes. Joey Giardello, he, the *numero uno* middleweight contender of the world floated high on life tonight. Already he was the proud father of a healthy boy at home and another born just five days ago. He was married to the cutest, sweetest girl in all of South Philly. *No sir. Heaven can't get any better than this.*

Joey stepped out of the car and walked toward the brightly lit front steps of the hospital, still humming "Amore" when he pushed through the lobby door. He knew that it had to be beyond late for visiting, but he desperately wanted to see his wife and recently newborn son. He wanted to share his happiness with them. The Tilellis had decided that if it was a boy, they'd name the child after himself. Carmine, but spell it differently: Carman. Joey was flat-out determined to see his wife and new child.

"Visiting hours ended ages ago. Go home. Come back after ten," said the duty nurse. "No way you're coming in here now!" She stood and puffed up her five-foot-two inch frame from behind the front desk. Joey stopped humming. He had to smirk to keep from laughing at the sight of this small, insignificant obstacle standing between him and his desire.

"No way yourself, I'm gonna see my boy and Rosalie." The

boxer's raspy, bass voice blasted down the halls and reverberated back almost as loud. He pounded his massive fist on the counter, rattling the glass top.

Later Rosalie would confess that she'd heard him causing a fuss that night and quietly laughed at his antics.

Across the lobby, a supervisor heard the commotion and walked behind the counter to where the duty nurse steadfastly held her ground. The supervisor had recognized the famous boxer and whispered into the nurse's ear. The nurse nodded slightly, and then lifted her chin. She glared back at Joey. "Okay. Okay ... IF ... *if* you quiet down. I'll take you to the nursery to see your son. But you can't disturb your wife—she needs her rest."

Joey nodded, accepting the deal. He followed her to the nursery. Soon he was looking through the glass at his son. He couldn't see much. A tiny pink bald head barely peeked out of a blue blanket tightly wrapped around the little body. Joey noticed that the neatly block-printed sign on the bassinet had the name "Tilelli" crossed out. Someone had grabbed a pen and scribbled "Giardello" under it.

Joey lowered his head and smiled contently. He felt a tug on his shirt from the impatient nurse. He looked down at her. He smiled again and meekly followed her to the front door. The roaring lion had been tamed, for the moment, by a docile, tiny wisp of a human; his second son, Carman, whom the world awaited.

Rubin "Hurricane" Carter, left, signs contract to fight Joey Giardello for the boxing middleweight crown in 1964 as an unidentified executive looks on. Denzel Washington played Rubin "Hurricane" Carter in the 1999 movie, The Hurricane. The film wrongly depicts the final round of the fight in which Carter is shown beating a defenseless Giardello. After Joey won a defamation of character lawsuit, the film's director, Norm Jewison, was required to state on the DVD that Giardello clearly won the fight.

1

The Hollywood Hurricane

January 11. 2000 • Cherry Hill, NJ

The reporter drove down the street slowly, nearly stopping in front of each house as he checked the numbers on the curb. As the black sedan crept past, one neighbor peeked out from behind parted curtains of her two-story, colonial house beyond a perfectly trimmed lawn. Finding the address, the guest pulled into the driveway of Carmine Tilelli, who had renamed himself Joey Giardello many years before, and his wife, Rosalie. Mr. and Mrs. Tilelli had moved into the house in 1962.

Viewed from the front, the style and upkeep didn't distinguish the place from any other property in the suburban environs. The custom-built, tri-level structure and an oversized backyard pool hinted that the owners may have been slightly more upscale than their neighbors during an earlier time. The home phone number had remained the same for nearly 40 years, and remained unconnected to voice mail or a fancy answering machine. It just rang if no one was home to pick up.

This family offered little clue as to their past public lineage. At this house, the Tilellis had raised four sturdy sons—Joseph, Carman,

Paul, and Steve. The first two, Joseph and Carman, were born and reared for a short time in South Philadelphia before the family's migration to southern New Jersey.

As he stopped and pulled up the emergency brake, Bernard Fernandez paused and wondered if the adjacent neighbors, or those directly across the street, knew the history of this quiet Italian-American family. Did any of these residents have a clue that they were living next door or across the street from two distinguished champions?

Nearly 10:00 a.m., Fernandez mused that by this time tomorrow, the neighbors would know at least half of the story—the "Joey Giardello" portion. The account about the household's other celebrity, Carman, the Special Olympian, would surely soon be retold too.

❋ ❋ ❋

In a semi-darkened Philadelphia movie house, Carmine Tilelli, who 35 years earlier had been known professionally as Joey Giardello, stared up at the huge wide-screen. He was dumbfounded, agitated. The proud 69-year-old man couldn't believe what his eyes had just absorbed, what had assaulted his ears. He couldn't remain still any longer. He shattered the quiet of the attentive audience: "NOOOOOO!"

Rosalie grabbed her husband's shoulder. With a finger to her lips, she whispered, "Shhhhhh," in an effort to calm him.

Movie viewers responded, "Be quiet!"

"Shut up!"

"Shhhhhh!"

"Yo, mouth!"

Joey had just watched the 20-foot-high image of actor Ben Bray portraying him as the world middleweight champion. There he was, leaning defenseless against the ropes, being pummeled by Rubin "Hurricane" Carter, played by Denzel Washington, in the biggest fight scene of the acclaimed movie, *The Hurricane*.

Only it didn't happen that way. Not at all. The film's deviation from the truth caused Joey to vent, to disturb the peace.

The scene allegedly depicted the 15th and final round of the 1964 title bout between Joey Giardello, the champion, and challenger Rubin "Hurricane" Carter. The film version fictitiously portrayed the last seconds of that round. In the scene, Denzel's "Hurricane" delivered eleven unanswered blows. After a few pawing responses Ben Bray's Joey tied up his opponent. After the referee quickly separated their clutching arms, "Carter" landed twelve more unreciprocated punches to the head and body. The weary, bashed and bloodied "Joey" took the punishment with hands down, defenseless. He somehow managed to stand upright until the bell ended the assault, the round, and the fight.

Film-goers then heard a ringside commentator announce above belligerent crowd rumblings: "It has taken 35 minutes for these judges to tell us what this hometown crowd already knows. Joey Giardello is about to lose the middleweight crown to Rubin 'Hurricane' Carter."

A bell clanged four times and the ring announcer finally blared out the verdict:

"LADIES AND GENTLEMEN. IT'S A
UNANIMOUS DECISION:
— THE WINNER AND STILL CHAMPION
— JOEY GIARDELLO. GIARDELLO!"

On screen, Joey's hometown, Philadelphia, fight crowd boos heartily, and the camera pans to disgruntled faces of ringside fans, reporters, and Denzel Washington mimicking a dejected Rubin "Hurricane" Carter. A blow-by-blow television announcer looks directly into the camera. "All I can say is that these Philadelphia judges must have been watching a different fight—because 'Hurricane' Carter took the fight."

During this sequence, Joey could barely keep his seat. He shook his head in disgust. "I don't believe this. This is a joke. He never hit me that much in *15* rounds," he quietly informed Rosalie.

Carmine and Rosalie were guests of the man who had pulled into their driveway hours earlier, *Philadelphia Daily News* sports reporter Bernard Fernandez. He had taken the "Giardellos" for a matinee screening of *The Hurricane*. Universal Studios promoted the film as "based on a true story," the troubled life of Rubin "Hurricane" Carter, a top middleweight contender who, in 1966, two years after the fight depicted in the movie, was accused and convicted of a triple homicide in Paterson, New Jersey. Carter was vindicated and released after 19 years in prison when a federal judge overturned the convictions. The judge "found a pattern of prejudice and racism" during the trials. This became the principal theme of the movie—a compelling story to say the least—especially as Carter's legal problems took place during the height of the Civil Rights movement, when equal rights and rioting dominated the evening news almost as much as the Vietnam War.

No matter how true the original story, Hollywood is well known for taking artistic liberties with particular scenes to create greater conflict, more trying situations, stronger motives and more lovable or more notorious characters. That's why they preface biopics like *The Hurricane* with the non-retractable "based on a true story." Studios do anything to create on-screen personae that can turn small films into successes, large-budget films into blockbusters. In *The Hurricane,* it was decided to spin the truth about the Giardello-Carter fight—suggesting that Giardello, who actually won a convincing, unanimous decision, was handed the fight—to play to the theme that drove the movie: eventual redemption from prejudice and racism. The Giardello-Carter fight scene provided additional evidence of racism for the plot in declaring Giardello the winner when the fight scene shows Carter beating Joey. What could be more racist than a black man being robbed of the decision and the championship title in the white man's hometown, the huge Philly boxing scene where the white man got his start and built his fame?

Rubin Carter's murder trials created a *cause célèbre*. Bob

Dylan and Jacques Levy wrote the song, "Hurricane," performed by Dylan in 1975 and featured throughout the movie:

Pistol shots ring out in the barroom night
Enter Patty Valentine from the upper hall.
She sees the bartender in a pool of blood,
Cries out, "My God, they killed them all!"

Here comes the story of the Hurricane,
The man the authorities came to blame
For somethin' that he never done.
Put in a prison cell, but one time he could-a been
The champion of the world.

In addition to Dylan, Muhammad Ali, Bill Bradley, Joni Mitchell, Ellen Burstyn, Stevie Wonder, Burt Reynolds, and Johnny Cash lent their names and/or donated money to Carter's defense cause. The *cause célèbre* became worthy indeed, as Carter was exonerated for murders that he always claimed he did not commit.

However, he didn't beat Giardello to a pulp in their fight, either. In reality, it was quite the opposite. Which is why, some 35 years after last being in the spotlight as one of the toughest fighters on the planet, Joey Giardello was about to re-enter the public eye. And it wasn't for just another 15 minutes of fame, nor for the money. No, sir—it was required to set the record straight and to reclaim his rightful legacy.

Joey devoted his life to his stellar boxing career, his mentally challenged son, and the rest of his family. He helped Eunice Shriver launch the Special Olympics and he raised thousands of dollars for St. John of God School for special-needs children. Joey had a proud legacy, which he felt he earned. Not solely a legacy based on his Hall of Fame boxing career, but outside the ring as well. His reputation had been tarnished by this movie. It had to be challenged and changed to reflect the truth. Joey was ready to do battle once again—this time against a powerful Hollywood studio.

❄ ❄ ❄

On the drive back to the Giardellos' Cherry Hill home, Joey lamented to Fernandez and Rosalie over the film's treatment of the actual fight of 35 years earlier. "Hon, I was never beaten like that movie showed, was I?" Joey asked Rosalie. He delivered the question more as a statement.

Rosalie, nearly as distraught as her husband, replied, "No. I couldn't believe what I saw. They made it seem like Carter beat the hell out of you. I was at the fight. It didn't happen that way."

"I don't want to, but I feel I have to ..." Joey's voice trailed a near whisper. "Sue somebody."

The next day's *Philadelphia Daily News* featured a full, tabloid-size, front-page photograph of Joey under the headline:

"THE REEL VICTIM GIARDELLO
INCENSED BY HOLLYWOOD'S PORTRAYAL
OF HURRICANE BOUT."

In the article, Fernandez told how Joey reacted during the fight scene with Carter and he quoted what Joey said about suing someone. Upon reading it, several Philadelphia lawyers immediately queued up, each seeking to be the first to call Joey.

Before the lawyers could begin their bombardment, Fernandez phoned his friend, boxing-savvy attorney George Bochetto, and asked him to call and consult with Joey. Thus, Bochetto earned the assignment to represent Giardello in a defamation of character civil action against Universal Studios and the film's worldwide distributors.

*Private Giardello, a "spit and polished" jump school graduate,
dresses in his class-A uniform for a 1947 photograph. In a full company
photograph, the U.S. Army spelled Joey's adopted name, "Giardelli."*

2

Street Fighter to Paratrooper to Married Pugilist

September 18, 1941 • Brooklyn, NY

Eleven-year-old Carmine "Chubby" Tilelli slouched down in his chair at the first of five rapid-fire bangs at the front door. His mother, two older, and two younger brothers looked immediately to Chubby. His father, Joseph Tilelli, pushed back from the dinner table and stomped past his wife and kids, out of the dining room. It was the fourth in a series of suppertime interruptions on this, the fourth day of the new school year.

A moment later, all remaining at the table heard the expected. "Chubby! Chubby come here!" Joseph's demanding voice was loud and fierce enough to scare the crap out of Superman. Carmine extricated himself from his chair then slowly walked toward the inevitable verbal thrashing and punishment that he knew awaited him.

At the front door, Carmine observed a man standing on the top step with his hand on the shoulder of a boy Carmine's age, but much taller and heavier. He recognized the boy. It was Robert, his victim *du jour.* Carmine's father glared at his son as he neared the doorway. When Carmine drew close enough, his father reached out and tugged on his shirt to hurry him along.

"Did you do this?" His father pointed toward the boy who stood outside, in the shadow of the heavy man cast by the dim porch light. The visiting boy sported a nasty black eye.

Knowing it was the schoolmate whom he'd fought earlier, Carmine answered softly. "Yes, Dad."

"Now apologize to Mister DiGirolamo and tell him that you won't hit his son again."

In an even weaker voice, Carmine offered, "Yes, Dad." He looked up. "Sir, I won't fight with Robert anymore."

"Thank you, Mr. Tilelli," said Robert's father. After securing Carmine's promise, the neighbors turned and stepped off the porch. Joseph Tilelli watched until the pair reached the sidewalk, then closed the door and turned off the outside light. Facing his son, Joseph frowned. "Chubby, why must you fight every day? Can't you play nice like your brothers?"

Carmine grew excited; this time, it appeared Dad wasn't going to punish him. "Dad, the big bully whuz hit'n on the cripple kid down the street. So I bopped him. Just one thump."

Carmine demonstrated for his father. He tightened his lips, made a fist, pulled his right hand back, then shot his left arm straight in front. It wasn't a slow, looping roundhouse, like the typical playground fight among boys, but a lightning-quick jab. Like a boxer.

Joseph Tilelli shook his head, placed his hand on his son's neck, squeezed lightly, and led him back to the dinner table. As they took their seats, the stern father thought, *My boy protected a handicapped child; that's not so bad. Fourth, fifth grade, kids fight; that's normal.* He wished though that Carmine didn't have to brawl each and every day, especially with neighborhood school companions. "Chubby must stay home all weekend. No baseball," announced the elder Tilelli to the rest of the family.

Punished again. Carmine opened his mouth to protest but thought better of the impulse. Missing baseball on Saturday really upset him. He loved to fight, but baseball was his game.

He dreamed of wearing the Brooklyn Dodgers' blue one day.

❋ ❋ ❋

A teenaged Carmine Tilelli, never far from a radio when his hero, Joe Louis, fought, leaned his ear closer to the Philco floor model radio speaker. He adjusted the four-way tone control to "deep."

Lewis became nearly every American's hero after he knocked out Nazi Germany's Max Schmeling in 1938. On a cold night in January, 1942, Carmine listened intently as the "Brown Bomber" KO'd Buddy Baer in the first round. Buddy, at 6-foot-6 the younger but taller brother of former heavyweight champ Max Baer, quipped a day after the fight: "The only way I could have beaten Louis that night was with a baseball bat."

Buddy Baer quit boxing for good after that fight and joined the Armed Services.

Meanwhile, Carmine just loved to fight. "As a kid, I always pictured myself a world champion, maybe even the heavyweight champ like Louis," he often remarked.

Carmine's father never did learn that a few years later, his wife, Anita, and his sister unknowingly aided and abetted the 13-year-old, always referred to as Chubby by family, in his quest to locate more worthy opponents than the current crop of Brooklyn, P.S. 203 seventh-grade classmates. Every Sunday, ferryboats cruised up and down the East and Hudson rivers around Manhattan, but one of them boarded groups of underprivileged kids. While Chubby was far from underprivileged, his aunt managed to sneak him on board, where he'd dash below deck, vault into a ring and fight the biggest, baddest competition available. The semi-organized, bare-knuckled bouts provided entertainment for the men huddled around the ring, who undoubtedly wagered on the fights. Those who put their money on Chubby Tilelli nearly always won.

By 1946, Carmine, now 15 ½ , grew tired of getting his hands dirty pulling axles and changing spark plugs during high school automotive shop training, so he quit school to join the Army. In order to enlist without parental approval, Carmine needed legal-age

ID. A friend knew someone, a cousin named Joseph Giardello, who would loan Carmine Orlando Tilelli legitimate papers. He borrowed the birth certificate and joined the 82nd Airborne Division. He bused to Fort Benning for basic and airborne training, then to Fort Bragg, N.C., where he morphed into Joey Giardello. Carmine Tilelli had planned to reclaim his legal name in two years when he mustered out of the service.

As it would turn out, the Joey Giardello deception lasted 21 years.

Immediately after enlisting, "Joey" reminded himself to call his parents and beg them to allow him to remain a proud Army paratrooper. His memory slipped for quite some time. It would be over a year before he called, as his father would relate many years later. Since, by then, Joey was almost old enough to enlist for himself, his father let him stay but asked the company commander to change the records to reflect his real name—Tilelli, not Giardello.

The amateur fighting career of Joey Giardello officially commenced in the Army, albeit reluctantly. Joey had watched his 17-year-old barracks buddy, Doug Walker, absorb a pretty good beating at the hands of a 22-year-old who had fought professionally before entering the Army. Joey didn't like the mismatch and asked his company commander if he could fight the ringer. Joey knocked the guy out in the first round. A full-bird colonel and longtime fight fan watched the bout in awe, his jaw dropping faster than Joey's opponent. Afterward, he approached Private Giardello and invited the trooper to join the regimental boxing team.

Joey fought a few times before quitting the team. He really only wanted to avenge his friend's beating. He professed to only a few fights while in the service, but Enrique Encinosa wrote in his 1984 book, *Boxing: This Is It!* that Giardello won two 82nd Airborne divisional boxing crowns. Doug Walker seconded Encinosa's claim. Never one to boast or enhance his accomplishments, many years later, Joey would hold on to his modest version of his Army boxing career.

However, his reluctance at climbing into the ring for structured rounds didn't prevent him from demonstrating his fighting prowess around the barracks, even though rules only allowed for open handed slap-boxing. "I was a pretty rough kid in the Army for a sixteen, seventeen-year-old. I didn't take no baloney from nobody," Giardello recalled.

A few North Carolina bar owners in the towns surrounding Fort Bragg discovered how best to put Joey's toughness to use: they hired him for bouncer duty. "Rough and tumble, everything I did."

On October 26, 1947, sixty members of the "Devils in Baggy Pants," dressed in Class-A uniforms, steel helmets, jump boots, and formal white gloves and traveled to New York City. They'd received the intimidating nickname from the Germans following their fierce fighting in the battle for the Italian port city of Anzio. In New York City, Joey Giardello proudly marched rifle high with fixed bayonet, a member of a 6,000-man honor guard representing all service branches for the returning European theatre's World War II Unknown Soldier. It was fitting that the 82nd Airborne be represented; it became known as "America's Guard of Honor" after General George Patton declared the unit "undoubtedly the best honor guard that I've ever seen."

Doug Walker, Giardello's Army buddy, described the somber event:

> We formed ranks at the New York docks in front of the flag-draped casket and caisson of the Unknown Soldier and proceeded on a very long and very solemn slow march up 5th Avenue and then on to Central Park. Once in Central Park, we led the Unknown Soldier into a large meadow where thousands of people were waiting, and there was a thunderous 21-gun salute. As we approached the narrow pathway, up toward the stands, as the cannon fire ended I thought I heard thousands of people laughing, but I soon realized it was thousands of special invited guests who lost loved ones during World War II and they were not laughing. They were understandably, shamelessly, crying, as I'm sure all of them thought that the returning Unknown Soldier could be their

loved one who was lost during the war. Truly a sound
I will never forget." (1)

Following the ceremony, the troops were dismissed in Central
Park, awarded a three-day pass, and proceeded to invade the bars
of New York. Joey readily showed Doug Walker *his town;* the two
proceeded to experience the time of their young lives. They were
stopped momentarily by a steep cover charge at the Century Room
of the Hotel Commodore until Bert Parks, star of "Stop the Music"
and future longtime host of the Miss America Pageant, observed
Joey holding out his empty pockets for all to see and assessed the
problem. Parks motioned for the *maître d'* to direct the soldiers to
join his table, which included Claudia Morgan, who played Nora
on *The Thin Man* radio show, and Don Wilson, best known as the
announcer-foil on the *Jack Benny Show*. Baritone Vaughn Monroe
finished a rendition of his theme song, "Racing with the Moon,"
and pulled up a chair next to Joey. Doug and Joey jumped at the
chance to dance with Parks' lovely wife, Annette. Money presented
no problem after joining the table of celebrities, as the whole group
taxied over to the Stork Club, honored to treat two members of the
82nd Airborne Division. The 82nd was one of the most decorated units
to fight in WWII, even though neither Joey nor Doug Walker had
joined in time to participate in the war.

After three days, the twosome managed to report back to the base
on time, but as Doug Walker described, they didn't look anywhere
near as "spit and polished" as when they had left. Fortunately for
them, General Patton wasn't around to see their returned condition as
he had regrettably died two years earlier, the result of an automobile
accident in Germany.

Subsequent to his airborne training jump school at Fort Benning,
Georgia, private Giardello headed north, where he landed at Fort
Bragg for his entire tour of duty. Joey parachuted 29 times before he
mysteriously left military life in early 1948 and migrated northward
to South Philadelphia, where he moved in with friends. Once again
he disappeared from his family in Brooklyn. Jobless and broke, he
sold his blood in order to eat.

Joey heard about a guy who arranged fights. He found the man, Jimmy Santore, and asked, "Can you get me a fight?"

Santore responded, "How many fights you had?"

"None." answered Joey.

"None! Well. I can get you some amateur bouts."

"Hey. I don't want to get hit for noth'n. I want to get paid!"

Santore liked Joey's cocky attitude. He directed him to a gym, and then, after a couple of days, on October 2, 1948, the 5-foot-10, 154-pound Giardello was driven over the Ben Franklin Bridge to New Jersey's state capital, Trenton. There, with little formal training, the 18-year-old climbed into a ring and did what General George Washington did to the Hessians and British the day after Christmas, 1776—he battered Johnny Noel quickly and decisively, winning his first bout by a second round knock-out. "I think that I was in there just to get smacked around. But I won!" Joey said after the fight. He earned $35 for the fight. "It was the easiest money I ever made."

Thus began the professional boxing career of Joey Giardello, who explained years later, "I used Giardello in case I got knocked out. I didn't want to ruin the Tilelli family name." Near the end of his boxing career he would wish that he'd remained a Tilelli in order to keep an important promise.

Rosalie Ropes a Ruffian

Seventeen-year-old, pretty, perky and petite birthday girl Rosalie Monzo turned off the radio just as Joe Grady, co-host of the popular "Grady and Hurst 950 Club" introduced Vaughn Monroe's latest number one single, "Ghost Riders in the Sky." She loved the recording but had to hurry out. Rosalie grabbed her coat and dashed to her Aunt Mamie's, who had promised to take her to the Earl Theatre to hear Frank Sinatra sing with the Tommy Dorsey Band.

On the way to Mamie's, Rosalie met Joey Giardello for the first time when he walked down Shunk Street with none other than her current boyfriend. They stopped to talk. She paid little attention to the muscular, curly-haired Giardello after they were introduced, but she must have caught Joey's eye, because the next time they met, he asked for her phone number. Imagine the nerve of Joey Giardello, a friend of her boyfriend, asking for her number.

She gave it to him.

He called.

For their first date, they attended a movie, *The Younger Brothers*. She disliked cowboy movies but felt tingly when Joey slipped his arm across her shoulder near the end of the rather short film. Rosalie even began to wish that the show would have lasted longer. On the way home, Joey told her that he had no family. He was all alone in the world. That attracted nurturing Rosalie even more.

Joey, somewhat a local celebrity because he boxed instead of working in a factory, at the shipyard, or any one of the many unglamorous jobs obtainable for most high school educated South Philadelphians, hung out with a bunch of guys at 13ᵗʰ & Shunk Streets, just a few blocks from Rosalie's home. Even her father, Paul, knew him. So it wasn't a big surprise when a week after the movie date, Joey invited Rosalie and her dad to his next fight.

The match, held at Toppi's just twelve blocks away from Rosalie's home, lasted only two rounds. Joey knocked out Henry Vonsavage for the win. Her dad was excited and told her that it was Joey's 14th fight and he'd never lost; better yet, it was his ninth KO. Dad was impressed. Rosalie was not. She had no interest in boxing. Her father left the arena right after the fight, but she waited for Joey to change; they walked home together. She tried to impress him with her new-found knowledge about his fight record. It must not have worked, because it took him almost a year to ask for her hand.

Rosalie answered in the affirmative and quickly planned a modest engagement party at her home. Rosalie thought her father seemed as happy as she. Paul Monzo loved Joey; as far as her mother, Jean, was concerned, Joey could do no wrong.

By the time of his engagement to Rosalie, Joey had fought 25 times and had suffered only one loss—unless you count the loss to the U.S. Army. After a bout in Washington, D.C., during the summer of 1949, it was discovered that Joey Giardello had shortchanged the 82ⁿᵈ Airborne Division by a few months on his two-year obligation. He flew back to Fort Bragg sans parachute to serve out the rest of his commitment. Years after his discharge, it was rumored that Joey had hit a sergeant who had wanted Joey to mow the lawn on a Sunday. All of a sudden Joey had gotten religious, refused to work, hit the non-com and walked away from the Army. His return to Bragg required time in the stockade before his release.

Rosalie's father thought little of the event, but she began to wonder about this guy whose name wasn't really Joey Giardello, who misrepresented his age to get into the Army, and then prematurely vanished from his military obligation. She also learned that he'd lied to her about not having family. His mother, father, and four brothers were alive and well in Brooklyn. Was this a portent of things to come? She wondered, but not enough to call off the engagement.

Once released from the Army, Joey sprang back into the ring after the four-month layoff and won a six-rounder in Philadelphia.

Joey and Rosalie were married just three weeks after the *damn Yankees* finished off her "Fighting Phillies." The Whiz Kids dropped four straight in the World Series. It didn't bother Joey much because he remained a loyal Brooklyn Dodgers fan. "Pee Wee Reese was my pal. He came over the house, gave me lots of balls and bats. I have the last glove 'Campy' (Roy Campanella, all-star hall of fame catcher) used. Baseball was my game."

Joey remained a Dodgers fan until the team moved to Los Angeles in 1957. He then began rooting for the hometown Philadelphia Phillies, although he maintained lifelong friendships with former Dodgers players Carl Furillo, who lived in nearby Reading, Pennsylvania, and Duke Snider, plus future coach and manager Tommy Lasorda.

By the beginning of the new decade, things were definitely looking bright for the rising young ring star. Joey traveled up to Brooklyn just three days before his October 29, 1950, wedding, only to lose his fight with Harold Green. Rosalie and Joey had slipped away before the church wedding, marrying in front of a justice of the peace on October 17, making sure that she wouldn't *officially* be marrying a guy who could be sporting a black eye to match his black tie.

Rosalie proved happy beyond her imagination but she couldn't help but wonder how life with a story-telling, raunchy, professional boxer would eventually turn out.

As was the custom for many young Italian couples in the early 1950s, Carmine and Rosalie Tilelli began their married life under the roof of her parents' South Philadelphia home until they saved enough money for a down payment on their own place.

Ominous Clouds Converge

On February 11, 1952, Rosalie gave birth to the couple's first son, Joseph, named not for the father's boxing alias but to honor the boy's paternal grandfather. By now, Giardello, only 22 years old, had raised his arm over 43 opponents, to go along with two draws and five losses. Already, he'd reached the half century mark in professional bouts. Though not yet considered a top contender for the middleweight crown, Joey's profile had shot well above the horizon with a win over a highly ranked Ernie Durando the previous April in Scranton, Pennsylvania.

A month shy of two years after Joseph's birth, second son Carman joined the family on January 30, 1954.

As Giardello's reputation heightened, he became a regular attraction at Madison Square Garden, New York, the undisputed Mecca for boxing matches. Three quick KO's at the Garden set rumors rumbling among the fight game's insiders that a title shot wasn't far away. The first in the series, Garth Panther, a crowding fighter who had never been knocked down before, fell in January. Walter Cartier tumbled in February. Rosalie had watched the fight from her hospital bed, but what she and the rest of the television audience missed was the action that transpired in the dressing room beforehand as told by Joe Rein, a former boxer:

"Joey was fighting in the main-go at the ol' garden.
I was in the dressin' room with a buddy who was on the

undercard. Cartier was a very intense guy—strapping shoulders and chest—trained religiously under the watchful eye of his twin brother at Stillman's Gym. He was an orthodox, stand-up boxer, with a solid right hand. And you could see, under his brother's encouragement, he believed that he could beat Joey and be vaulted into the title picture. He was gettin' his game face on. All of a sudden, the locker door burst open. It's Giardello in an outrageously expensive camel's hair coat tied at the waist—surrounded by an army of *goombahs*—some with cigars in their yaps, spillin' into the room. All commotion and noise. Joey strode over to Cartier, whose mouth was agape, and gave'm a big slap on the back, "HOW YA DOING WALTER!" The blood drained from Cartier's face. The TKO in the first round was a formality: Walter lost it in the dressing room. (2)

Then in March, Joey knocked out rising star Willie Troy in the seventh round.   Look out middleweight division; Giardello just served notice that his punches packed a thump to go with his ring caginess.

Joey's managers were Carmine Graziano and Tony Ferrante, the latter a nephew of notorious mob guy Antonio "Tony Bananas" Caponigro. "Bananas must have made a lot of money off Joey's three fights at the Garden because they sent us to Florida for a fully-paid vacation," said Rosalie. "Tony Bananas scared me. He came over the house once, a big man, wear'n a big black coat, a black hat, and arrives in a big black car. He scared me. I went upstairs. Let them (Joey and Bananas) talk." She never asked what they talked about, either.

The meeting may have had nothing to do about boxing, as Joey had recently lost a $200 bet on his beloved Dodgers and needed a "swing loan" until his next payday. Joey had a different take on Bananas. "I trust Tony Bananas more than I do the New York Athletic Boxing Commission," Joey once told a *Sports Illustrated* reporter.

"At least he's a man of his word. When he tells you something, at least you know it's going to be so."

It is certain Bananas never informed Joey about his future plans for Philadelphia mob boss Angelo Bruno. Bananas was alleged to have plotted and even personally executed the unsanctioned hit on Angelo Bruno in March of 1980. This killing would ignite a Philadelphia mob war that would lead to its eventual demise as an underworld power in Philadelphia.

A few weeks after the Bruno killing, Tony "Bananas" Caponigro was found dead in the trunk of a car with dollar bills stuffed in his mouth—a mob shorthand for greed.

✳ ✳ ✳

The euphoria that Joey felt after his seventh-round knockout of Willie Troy soured the very next day though, as soon as he walked in the door after his long drive home from New York City. Rosalie had become deeply disturbed about Carman. The doctor had come by the day before and instructed her to practice feeding Carman with an eye dropper because he couldn't suck on a bottle like their first son or any *normal* baby. Joey thought it strange but let it slide.

However, if Rosalie had a worry, Joey owned it too.

After the Florida vacation, things started to snowball. At training camp, Joey violated the "no baseball" rule and tore up a knee sliding into second base.

Then a more urgent issue concerning Joey's boxing career surfaced. Rumors routinely fly wild around boxers' training camps, but Joey heard one that started with his name and ended with the current champion of his middleweight division: "Giardello's *not* getting the match with Bobo Olson."

At the press conference for his May 21st bout with Pierre Langlois, Joey heard confirmation of the rumor: Rocky Castellani would be next to challenge Olson for his title.

A week before the Langlois fight, Joey was completely unsettled about recent events. He went out drinking with his buddies. One friend cautioned him: "Joey, you're fighting in a couple of days;

take it easy on the sauce." Joey retorted, "No title shot, bad leg, something's wrong with Carman—I need a drink."

That Friday night, he lost the Langlois fight and fell deeper into self-pity and self-loathing. Days later, Joey lamented, "Langlois. I beat him two years ago. I shouldn't have lost that fight. He couldn't break an egg with two fists, but he knocked me down and won the fight."

❀ ❀ ❀

At home, Rosalie tussled with another weighty matter: after almost five months, Carman still couldn't sit up. She knew something wasn't right. The doctors told her that she shouldn't expect Carman to be as fast at doing things as her first son. Rosalie's obstetrician had told her pediatrician not to inform her that anything was wrong with Carman because he feared that his diagnosis might be devastating for Joey. The obstetrician had good intentions—he didn't want to alarm Joey because he had heard that Joey might soon be getting a title bout. Rosalie didn't know the nature of the problem, but she knew that *Carman was not right* and she worried. Joey stored that worry far behind his own, even losing his heralded fighting career-centered focus.

Distressed about Rosalie's concerns over Carman, his leg, and the apparent lost title shot, Joey sought relief. He went AWOL again, this time from his Summit, New Jersey, training camp. A friend, Bobby Patrone, drove him a hundred miles to Atlantic City for a night on the town. During their return drive early the next morning, Patrone steered into the median. The car rolled over three times. Asleep in the back seat, Joey was not badly hurt but he had to be dragged out of the car by Patrone. A third man, Vincent DiFillipps, also asleep in the back seat, had more serious injuries.

As they flopped in the median beside the upside down car, Bobby Patrone told Joey that he didn't have a license, so Joey replied, "Tell the troopers that I was driving." That magnanimous offer would come back to kick Joey in the rear before year's end. Newspapers across the country carried the wire-service story that Joey was driving, but he denied being behind the wheel.

While Joey wasn't seriously hurt, word leaked out that he was near death. Both his wife and father heard a faulty news report before he was able to contact them. Joey's father nearly suffered a heart attack.

On September 24th, Joey fought Ralph "Tiger" Jones on one leg and somehow won a 10-round decision. "I beat Jones but I couldn't make any sharp turns. I was hurting," Joey recalled. He realized that it was impossible to continue fighting without surgery. He cancelled an upcoming scheduled bout and proceeded to St. Agnes Hospital in Philadelphia on October 5. Right after the operation a news photographer took a picture of Joey in a wheelchair flanked by two widely smiling nuns. Surgery, lost income, and Carman's circumstances further lowered the now top-ranked contender's already depleted morale.

Five days after successful surgery, while still in the hospital, Joey's spirit got a big lift when middleweight champion Bobo Olson's camp announced a December 15th title fight with Giardello in San Francisco.

Only a day later his spirit crashed again when he read a newspaper report that New York boxing commissioner and chairman of the International Boxing Commission's championship committee, Bob Christenberry, challenged the bout. He stated. "How silly can they get? They announce a title match for a contender who is in a hospital. The sports pages are filled with pictures of Giardello in a wheelchair." The commissioner also claimed that Pierre Langlois should get the fight over Giardello and that he'd have more to say about the match at the London meeting. "We may refuse to recognize it as a title fight. We may refuse to recognize Giardello as the top challenger."

In Philadelphia, Giardello's co-managers, Anthony Ferrante and Carmen Graziano (no relation to Giardello's good friend and former boxer, Rocky Graziano, whose legal name was Thomas Rocco Barbella), both claimed that Giardello would be in perfect shape for the proposed nationally televised 15-round event. Joey reminded his managers that it was commissioner Christenberry who changed a judge's card after the infamous 1952 Graham/Giardello split-decision fight, giving the win to Graham. Giardello had sued, and the New York Supreme Court overturned the ruling in favor of Giardello. (3)

Despite her husband's mounting legal and physical problems, Rosalie began her quest for answers to Carman's condition.

(1) *Biography of a Bowhunter* by Doug Walker, 2008
(2) Joe Rein, former boxer, executive editor, *FightBeat.com*
(3) Giardello/Graham bout Madison Square Garden. NY, NY, December 15, 1952. Source: AP wire service story February 17, 1953, Justice Bernard Botein decision.

Philadelphia Phillies' mascot the "Philly Phanatic" makes a big mistake challenging the champion to a few rounds before a game. This action took place at the old Veterans Stadium in South Philadelphia, a short distance from where the 1954 "Riot on Broad Street" gasoline station was located.

3

The Broad Street Riot

The Civil War ended in 1865, but hostilities between north and South Philadelphians erupted in the mid-1950s in the form of racial animosity, mistrust, and open hatred. The violence predated the height of the Civil Rights struggle by a decade.

As factory mills closed and jobs vanished, residents of English, Irish, Polish, and German ancestry vacated their homes sandwiched between the Schuylkill and Delaware Rivers north of Market Street, a definable Philadelphia north/south boundary. Large populations of the Frankford, Fishtown, and Kensington neighborhoods resettled in the Pennsylvania/New Jersey suburbs, where brand-new track homes in places like Levittown and Cherry Hill promised "the good life"—for Caucasian applicants. Negro buyers filled the void created by the "white flight," causing housing prices in the racially changing Philadelphia neighborhoods to plummet. The size of the African-American communities expanded still more rapidly.

Even the Philadelphia School Board exhibited blatant racism when it voted to move the location of its proud namesake—Northeast High School—when the neighborhood began tilting toward black and Hispanic. (1)

Ironically, it appears that the School Board may have delayed the move of Northeast High School by six months until the graduation of a guaranteed "can't miss," future all-pro, Hall-of-Fame football player, Herb Adderley. The school board members wanted to claim the trophies he helped to accumulate and move them to the new, whiter neighborhood. The trophies were moved to a new school building located at 1601 Cottman Avenue, much farther north and east, culturally, of 8th & Lehigh Avenue than in distance. Adderley is perhaps the second most successful, popular, and famous black athlete to hail from a Philadelphia High School. The most legendary, no doubt, was Wilt Chamberlain. (2)

In South Philadelphia, the mostly ethnic Italian neighborhoods stayed intact and remained solid white, solid Italian. Philadelphia's center city commercial and business district served as a buffer between the antagonistic black and white communities.

The "Bad Boy of Boxing" earns his reputation

During this racially tense time on October 28, 1954, Joey Giardello motored along Broad Street late at night with two tipsy pals only hours after being released from the hospital on crutches. The South Philly celebrity stopped for gas. Unfortunately, the service station he chose conducted business directly across the street from one of Father Devine's "Heavens" at Broad and Catharine Streets in South Philadelphia.

Father Devine, aka George Baker, had purchased a grandiose, turn-of-the-century, ten-story hotel in 1948 on north Broad Street where he shepherded what might be called a bi-racial cult today, whites and blacks cohabitating in a religious, community service-oriented facility.

The organization's rules were strict: No smoking, no drinking, and no profanity. The men and women lived on separate floors. The 10th floor was designated a place of worship, and the ground floor served as a dining area where meals were distributed to a needy public for as little as twenty-five cents.

Whatever the good intentions of Father Devine, it was more than

Joey Giardello's drunken passengers could stomach when they saw whites and blacks leaving one of his facilities together.

Giardello asked the colored service attendant, Howard Short, for three dollars' worth of gas. One of Joey's passengers yelled out the window at the people across the street: "Look at them sons-of-bitches over there. Those white trash with those Niggers."

Joey looked up at the service attendant. "Don't mind them. They've been drinking."

The attendant responded with a derogatory remark, one that Giardello would refuse to repeat in front of a jury months hence. Joey's passengers, Joseph Bonadies and Victor Mariani, heard it though, and bolted out of the car. Bonadies grabbed Giardello's crutch from under the back seat. It thumped against Joey's head. Near the pump, Howard Short ducked a Bonadies punch and swung a water bucket in defense. Short was then struck by the crutch. Giardello yelled for his two friends to get back in the car; when they did, Joey drove away without retrieving the crutch or paying for the gas.

As they cleared the driveway, heading south onto Broad Street, a tire iron thrown by a second attendant crashed against the trunk of Joey's sparkling new Oldsmobile.

Attracting a crowd back at a Moore and Hicks South Philly bar, Giardello and his passengers dramatized their adventure, while knocking down a few more beers. "I never went to this bar before and I never had known this Victor Mariani," lamented Giardello years later. A number of guys meandered out to view the damage to Joey's car and suggested a return, "pay back" trip to the gas station. Joey originally declined, but later relented. A dozen patrons piled into four cars and headed to the service station for retribution.

A wide-eyed Howard Short observed the angry motorcade screech to a halt in front of the service station's office. Short, station owner Frank Gallo, his wife, and the other attendant huddled together in the locked office as the mob hammered on the door. Short had called Gallo after the first incident.

Giardello parked on the street a half block away and then hobbled on one crutch, trying to catch up with the group. Bonadies smashed the station's office window and opened the door. The gang rushed in with Mariani waving a gun—or a starter pistol, as Giardello would later allege. Unable to catch up to the rest of the gang, Giardello limped back to his car for a quick departure. "I heard banging on my window and the guys with me are running around, so I beep my horn," he remembered. "'Come on!' They get in. I make a U-turn and get away from there. But a cab driver saw me; he must have taken my plate number and called the cops." By now all the bars were closed, so the hooligans headed for an after-hours club to compare notes and celebrate.

Joey, blissfully unaware that the police were looking for him, reveled in the company of his co-conspirators plus a few adoring, drunken, barfly fans.

❊ ❊ ❊

Rosalie, long asleep at home with her two young boys, had no idea how much trouble her "ringleader" husband had instigated this night.

She heard her oldest son cry. *He must have had a bad dream.* She glanced at the alarm clock: It was after three. *Where's Joey?* Rhetorical question. She struggled out of bed and comforted Joseph. Before she left the spare bedroom that served as the nursery, she looked in the crib at Carman. *This little one, he sleeps all night and all day.* She felt guilty that he slept so much and caused so little trouble. She constantly, ceaselessly worried about her undersized, slow-to-learn, double-jointed, sweet, slanty-eyed Carman.

As she walked back to the bedroom, Rosalie bit her lip and shook her head, remembering something strange the pediatrician had asked. He wanted to know if anyone else in the family had slanty eyes. She answered that she thought an aunt in Joey's family did.

❊ ❊ ❊

Two cops walked into the after-hours club, approached Joey, and ordered him to come with them. Joey asked why; they told him he'd find out downtown. A number of Joey's companions said, "We were with him," and offered to go along to the station house.

"No," the cops said. "We just want Joey."

The groupies piled into their cars and followed anyway.

At the police station, the officers presented Joey by his real name, Carmine Tilelli, to Howard Short. They asked if he was the man who hit him.

"No," the gas station attendant answered.

The cops took advantage of the uninvited crowd that followed Joey and lined them up for Short. He picked out a couple of guys, including Victor Mariani, whom the attendant claimed waved a gun in his face.

The cops explained to Joey that the owner wanted $1,000 to fix the window. Assuming that it would become a civil case, the cops released everybody. Joey said that personally, he wouldn't pay anything. He told the guys to pony up for the damage then quickly forgot about the whole incident. Perhaps financial restitution would have put an end to Giardello's participation in The Broad Street Riot. Unfortunately, nobody contributed a dime to pay the service station owner for the damages. The issue remained unresolved.

After a few weeks at home, Joey, convinced that he could rehab in time for the Olson championship fight, went off to training camp. It didn't take long at camp, though, before he realized that he just wouldn't be able to get into shape and train properly by mid-December to fight. "I couldn't do nothing. I couldn't put weight on my leg. I just couldn't do nothing. So I told my managers, 'Call off the fight.' I was getting a hundred thousand for the fight. I said, 'Call it off.'" His managers notified the Olson camp. The fight was cancelled. Joey returned home to Rosalie and their two boys.

The DA Books the Boxer

By late November, weeks after Giardello had regretfully notified the Bobo Olson camp that he couldn't prepare in time for the December15 fight, he turned his attention on Carman. He and Rosalie pressed their pediatrician for answers. Reluctantly, the doctor told them that Carman was mentally retarded and that he probably wouldn't progress beyond the mental abilities of a seven-year-old. Rosalie became distraught. She cried. The couple, not satisfied with that response, took Carman to a few more local doctors hoping for a different diagnosis and a more promising prognosis. They received neither.

A month after the gas station riot, at seven in the evening on November 28, Joey drove to a private club in center-city Philadelphia. The doorman delayed him long enough to say that Police Inspector John Driscoll was looking for him. After strutting to the bar and ordering a drink, Joey walked downstairs to use a public phone. He called the Inspector, whom he knew well, and asked if he wanted him. Driscoll told him no, but asked where he was, just in case. Joey informed the Inspector that he was at the SA Club, Broad and Locust.

Joey hung up the phone and walked back upstairs. By the time he reached the bar, two officers with shotguns awaited him. A few minutes later, Inspector Driscoll arrived. A stunned Giardello asked. "John, what the hell's going on here? What's with the guns?"

"It's about the gas station assault," Driscoll explained. "Let's go." He and the officers escorted Joey to police headquarters.

There, the district attorney and current mayoral candidate Richardson Dilworth awaited the boxer. Dilworth booked Joey Giardello for the assault and battery of Howard Short on October 29, 1954. When Joey had been hauled in for questioning by the police in October, he had only been identified by his legal name, Carmine Tilelli. When the DA's office discovered that the leader of the hooligans was actually the famous middleweight contender, Joey Giardello, "The Broad Street Riot," became a more significant case.

Ironically, on the day of Giardello's booking for a "hate crime," as it would have been defined by the Hate Crime Statistics Act of 1990, it was announced that actor Tony Curtis had been awarded the George Washington Carver Institute's "Outstanding Contributions to Racial Unity" in Hollywood. Curtis was feted for his assistance in organizing youth clubs to combat delinquency and for sponsorship of libraries in Negro schools.

District Attorney Dilworth saw to it that Giardello was relieved of his Pennsylvania boxing license and released him on bail. He was told not to leave Philadelphia. Later, at a preliminary hearing, a trial date was set for February 14, 1955.

On December 22, Vincent DiFillipps, the seriously injured passenger in the August automobile accident on the Garden State Parkway, decided to sue Giardello for his pain and suffering. He sought $100,000—the exact amount Joey lost by cancelling the Olson championship fight.

As if the lawsuit wasn't a sufficiently sour note on which to end the year, Joey added to his own plight. On December 28, he was arrested once again, along with his brother Robert, for disorderly conduct and interference with an officer. The next day, Magistrate Elias Myers suspended the charges but couldn't resist admonishing the number one middleweight contender: "Joey, I never saw anyone who threw a million dollars away before. You're discharged." The magistrate presumably referred to the lost income from future bouts as middleweight champion because of Giardello's skirmishes outside of the ring.

Joey got lucky. A guilty charge could have caused his bail to be revoked. District Attorney Dilworth would have unceremoniously sent him to jail where he would have remained until the scheduled February assault and battery trial.

Only two days remained until the New Year. Joey sat at home and pondered how in the world nineteen hundred and fifty-four could have ended so badly after such a promising start. He bemoaned his difficulties: gimpy leg, auto accident, cancelled championship fight, upcoming criminal trial, lost boxing license, lost income, DiFillipps' hundred-thousand-dollar lawsuit ... and ... and something's definitely ailing Carman.

(1) Northeast High School physically moved from 8th and Lehigh in 1957. The facility was then renamed Thomas A. Edison High School. In 1988 Edison High moved to a new facility. Edison High School possesses the dubious honor of having the most students (66) killed in the Vietnam War. Source: Edison High School website.

(2) Wilt Chamberlain graduated from Philadelphia's Overbrook High School, 1955. Source: Overbrook High School year book. Herb Adderley, designated All Pro five times, starred at cornerback for the Green Bay Packers during their dominating run through the NFL in the 1960s, which included the first two Super Bowl championships. Source: Pro Football Hall of Fame records.

Joey taught Carman to ice skate on their backyard pool. Carman, a natural athlete, played baseball and football and later became a Special Olympics gold-medal runner.

4

"What's Wrong With My Son?"

With clanking bell, the driver of a rumbling trolley car stopped to discharge his passengers. The car's folding steps dropped with a thud. The trolley's racket mixed with the constant din of slow-moving automobiles. These sounds were the only disturbance of a silence that hung between Joey and Rosalie, as they made the long drive from South Philly, north on 63rd Street toward Wynnewood, the suburban Philadelphia location of Lankenau Hospital.

Joey sat up straight, head forward, fully concentrating on his task: Eyes locked onto the car immediately ahead, both hands tight to the wheel, an uncustomary, stiff driving position for him.

Rosalie's eyes wandered out the passenger window as the city's row homes eventually gave way to tree-lined suburban streets. The homes were now spaced far apart, many with front lawns where small children played. Some yards were surrounded with chain link fences, eliminating a parent's fear of street traffic. For a fleeting moment, Rosalie envisioned her two sons playing in such a yard, with the youngest, Carman, racing older brother Joseph across a manicured green expanse. A fleeting smile escaped her tightened lips.

Alone with their thoughts, each wished for, if not a miracle, then at least the hope that this doctor, this specialist, could provide a better prognosis for Carman's condition than those offered by the Philadelphia doctors. Those doctors had all said that there was no treatment, no cure for *mongolism.*

Joey had read about "The Physician of the Year," Doctor Spitz, a renowned pediatric neurosurgeon at Lankenau Hospital whose intelligence could never be fully measured. He finished his medical training by age twenty-five—three to five years ahead of the norm.

Whether Joey and Rosalie were fully aware of the doctor's pedigree or not, they had found for Carman arguably the best available physician in the country. Carman was taken to the hospital for testing, and remained there under Dr. Spitz's scrutiny for four days.

The Tilellis, like many other couples in their mid-twenties the proud parents of two children, sat in Dr. Spitz's office anxiously waiting for him to look up from his papers. The delay added to their anxiety. When his eyes finally lifted to Joey, then Rosalie, they simultaneously exhaled, releasing a minuscule amount of the tension that stretched their taut facial muscles. Finally, they would hear what the battery of tests revealed and the prognosis for Carman's future.

The well-tanned, prematurely balding 36-year-old doctor leaned forward over his desk. "I don't have good news." He paused. Rosalie slumped noticeably in her seat. Joey lowered his head, looked down at the floor, and waited.

The doctor went on, "Carman has Down syndrome. This is a genetic disorder caused by an extra chromosome. Carman has forty-seven instead of the normal forty-six."

Joey looked up and raised his shoulders; a silent response.

"There is no treatment for Down syndrome." Now the doctor inhaled deeply. He began speaking at a rapid pace. "And since you already have another child, I'm afraid that Carman will cause conflict in the home, so I strongly suggest that you place Carman in an institution for the mentally retarded. I can suggest a very good one right here in Philadelphia."

The Tilellis bolted upright as if both had been slapped across the face. Bewildered by the medical jargon and shocked by the blunt suggestion that they should deposit Carman in an institution, each stared at the doctor mutely.

Rosalie wanted to strike back at the person who had spoken those confusing, offensive words. Joey was bewildered and angry. *All this time, four days and the money—forget about the money—but all this time and he tells us Carman has an incurable condition and we should just send him away.* Joey looked to Rosalie, then to his watch as though he had a more urgent place to be. He rose up, his jaw locked in disgust. Rosalie stood when her husband did.

Dr. Spitz looked puzzled. He was accustomed to ending the sessions, not following suit. He got up from his seat and walked to the front of his desk.

Joey managed to thank the doctor and extended his hand. Realizing that the couple had no comments or questions, Dr. Spitz held onto Joey's hand longer than necessary. "I know this is difficult for you, but please, please strongly consider my advice." He let go of the hand. "Call me when you've had time to think it over. I know how hard this is for you and Rosalie. But trust me. Carman will cause conflict. Call, I'll make arrangements with the facility in advance for you."

Dr. Spitz wished them both well and quietly directed the Tilellis out of his office. He pointed to an assistant, who led Joey and Rosalie to a nursery, where they collected Carman.

Rosalie held their son tightly, fearful that he might magically fly out of her arms directly to some cold, dismal institution for the retarded. Rosalie reviewed word for word what the doctor had said. She wanted to be sure that she had fully understood. Satisfied with her recollection, she could only keep repeating the phrase, *"He'll cause conflict in the home."* But despite the horrible news that he had delivered and his ridiculous suggestion, Rosalie sensed a genuine concern from the doctor.

Joey and Rosalie walked hurriedly away from the hospital to their car. All the way home they questioned each other. "What did the doctor mean when he said Carman would cause conflict in the home?" Rosalie wanted to know.

Joey had no answer. He wanted to know more about Down syndrome. "What's a chromosome? What's it got to do with Carman's intelligence and how will it affect his ability to learn?"

Rosalie wondered why they hadn't stayed and asked the doctor for the answers to their questions. She guessed that Joey was just too upset after he told them to send Carman to a place that she envisioned as a place for the mentally insane.

They rained question upon question on each other, neither able to supply answers. But they knew one thing: The thought of sending Carman away to an institution for the retarded?

Never!

Once home, they called their parents with the news. Later, Rosalie walked a block away to share the devastating report with her friend, Mrs. Avallone —mother of teen idol, Frankie Avalon, whose recording of "Venus" would top all the charts four years later. He'd also star along with a former Mouseketeer, Annette Funicello, in three highly popular Malibu Beach movies. The Tilellis and the Avallones would both move to Cherry Hill, New Jersey, a decade later and become neighbors once again.

Not knowing any more about Carman's condition and prognosis after the battery of tests by Doctor Spitz than she did beforehand, Rosalie decided that she would have to learn how to raise him on her own as she went along.

Joey added the burden of Carman's uncertain future to the weighty problems already heaped upon his muscular but noticeably sagging shoulders. He wondered how this could have happened to him, a virile, sturdy, modern Italian gladiator. *How could I have produced a retarded child? I didn't smoke much. Yeah, maybe I drank too much beer. Nah, the doctor would have said something if booze caused it.*

He couldn't help but wonder if it was possible that the extra chromosome came from Rosalie's side. Publicly, he professed bravado, but privately he wondered how much more his psyche could take.

Like Rosalie, Joey would hear all kinds of opinions and advice on how best to care for Carman. He, like his wife, would consider all options but one: placing Carman in a home for the mentally retarded.

Dr. Spitz went on to pioneer life-saving surgery for children with hydrocephalus—a dangerous buildup of spinal fluid in the brain. He also developed surgeries to remedy brain tumors and epilepsy in children. He treated youngsters from all over the world. Despite his fame and accomplishments, he was described as a humble man by colleagues. He died at age 87 in 2005. (1)

(1) *Philadelphia Inquirer. 12/19/05*

Author's note: Dr. Eugene Bernard Spitz's suggestion to place Carman in an institution was the prevalent medical advice during the 1950s and the retelling here is not meant as a personal criticism, nor meant to defame this extraordinary man and his many accomplishments.

A top middleweight boxing contender during most of his career, Joey Giardello realized his dream of becoming champ in 1963 when Dick Tiger of Nigeria offered him a title bout. Giardello had to dress appropriately for his few bouts in the courts.

5

The Trial and Trying Times

The "Riot in Philly" trial was moved from February 14 to April 4, 1955, by Joey Giardello's lawyers, despite strong opposition by the prosecutors. That team, led by District Attorney and Philadelphia mayoral candidate Richardson Dilworth, argued that Giardello delayed the trial so that it wouldn't start until after his championship fight with Carl Bobo Olson, rescheduled from the previous December to March 24. Should Giardello win the belt, the prosecutors claimed that he believed that no judge would place the world middleweight champion behind bars.

Dilworth elaborated. "The word has spread that this man will never come to trial. They say that the fix is in, and if he becomes champion, we couldn't try him."

Judge Reimel allowed the continuance to April 4, stating that if convicted in February, Giardello would surely miss an opportunity to fight for the championship even though a conviction could be overturned on appeal. Successfully arguing for the continuance was attorney Michael van Moschzisker, a former first assistant to DA Dilworth.

Extremely disturbed by the delay, Dilworth sarcastically told the press. "Giardello's method of training is to stand outside saloons and trip up people as they come by. If they object, he beats them up." (1)

Prejudicial statements like this had led some to conclude that Dilworth was campaigning for Negro votes in the upcoming November election by tenaciously prosecuting the white boxer for allegedly hitting Negro service attendant Howard Short. By Joey's recollection, Mr. Short had already stated to police on the night of the incident that Joey was not the one who had struck him with a crutch.

The prosecution offered to drop the gun charge against Victor Mariani, the pistol waver, if Mariani's memory might "improve" over his first account of the incident.

If the "fix" was in, as the DA suggested, it now appeared that the prosecution had secured a guilty verdict with the promises of less than truthful testimony even before trial began.

Joey and his lawyers had to fight on three fronts: the criminal assault charges, to reinstate Joey's license with the Pennsylvania boxing commission, and to defend against the $100,000 civil suit launched by the seriously injured Vincent DiFillipps after the automobile accident.

Successful in getting his travel ban removed by early 1955, Giardello was able to secure licenses and fights in Norfolk, Virginia, in January; Miami Beach, Florida, in February; and Milwaukee, Wisconsin, in March. He won all three bouts, the last a KO of Germany's top middleweight contender, Peter Mueller, in 29 seconds of the second round. "Olson knows I'm looking for him," Giardello stated after the Mueller fight.

However, Olson's camp now went on record declaring that the champ wouldn't defend the belt against Giardello until after the trial. Joey's co-manager, Tony Ferranti, noted, "The trial comes up in two weeks," implying that Giardello would be found not guilty and that Olsen should keep his fight schedule open.

❋ ❋ ❋

On the home front, Joey and Rosalie's oldest son, Joseph,

entered the "terrible twos"; fortunately, he was anything but terrible. baby Carman still slept for many hours during the day plus all night, as he was barely able to sit up, eat solid food and crawl. Potty training would take Rosalie another four years to complete with him. Learning to talk would take even longer. Rosalie persevered, having never seen or known a retarded child, or one who was "feeble-minded," as she heard behind her back. She learned to care for Carman on her own. Rosalie never gave up or grew impatient with Carman's painfully slow progress.

She also made sure that first-born Joseph received as much attention as Carman. She became determined to treat each son with identical measures of love and affection, never slighting either. And, more importantly, she was even more resolute to scold and punish both with equal justice under *Rosaliean* law.

She held tightly onto Dr. Spitz's statement, never forgetting that he predicted Carman would cause conflict in the home. While she never quite understood what he meant, she steeled herself to assure that any conflict caused by her second son would never take up residence in her home.

Joey's mounting problems, including the loss of his Pennsylvania boxing license, a possible lost championship opportunity, his endangered boxing career, and the prospect of incarceration caused Rosalie great anguish and many sleepless nights. However, the slight, 95-pound woman never passed along her personal dread onto her husband's perfect, 160-pound, fighting-weight frame.

The trial date switched again, this time earlier, now that the championship fight had been officially called off. Court proceedings began on Monday, March 14, 1955. The trial lasted three days. As Joey's defense team expected, the accuser, gasoline service attendant Howard Short, testified that Giardello had been the one who had hit him with the crutch. Relieved that the gun charges were dropped from his indictment, Victor Mariani corroborated Short's accusation.

Giardello took the stand in his own defense and stated: "I never hit Mister Short with my crutch. I tried to be the 'peace maker' during the whole affair." He related that Mister Short had called him a nasty name, one which he wouldn't repeat in front of the judge and jury even in the cause of his own defense. But he emphatically denied that he acted upon it. "I never even got out of the car," he added.

The jury of seven women and five men took five hours to reach a verdict. As the foreman repeated "guilty" after each of five charges. Giardello stood in silence, stunned. Judge Edward Little released Giardello into the custody of his attorney, Michael van Moschzisker, while the lawyer filed an appeal for a new trial and made arrangements for a bail hearing. Giardello faced up to eight years in prison and was required to pay a $3,500 fine.

Having falsely believed that he'd never be found guilty, Giardello finally had to deal with the severity of his situation—up to *eight years in prison*. He silently repeated the phrase over and over in his head as van Moschzisker directed him out of the courtroom on wobbly legs ... the same legs that normally stood firm as tree trunks, even after ten rounds with the toughest, stiffest of opponents. The minimum sentence could be probation, but nobody in Joey's camp was counting on that possibility. They believed that DA Dilworth, now Philadelphia's leading candidate for mayor, would be working overtime behind the scenes to make sure that probation never happened.

(1) Philadelphia, PA. UPI, Feb. 4, 1955

Joey idolized the Brooklyn Dodgers, here gathered in Joey's South Philly kitchen enjoying a brew or two (left-to-right) 1950-era players: Dick Williams, Duke Snider, Carl Erskine, Pee Wee Reese and Clem Labine.

6

The DA Offers a Deal

The freshly paved street lacked the signs of routine use or a laid "patch" after a Chevy Bel Air hotrod's jackrabbit start. The newly poured concrete sidewalks had yet to feel a little girl's hand chalk etching of a hopscotch court. The smooth new-brick facades of the houses reflected sunlight back onto the street, making the parked cars appear as shiny as the day they had left the dealers' showrooms. Joey and Rosalie had purchased one of these brand-new, never-occupied, South Philly homes. The property cost $10,400; Joey thought that he easily could afford it. Situated just a few blocks from Rosalie's mom and dad, the place offered the prospects of a happy life for the family, if not for all the heavy, toxic baggage Joey lugged with him.

As 1955 dragged on, the pressures inside Giardello redlined like a steam boiler gauge ready to burst. The heaviest load was the prospect of hard time in prison, but his entire life was on hold—no boxing, no income, no future. He also worried over Carman's condition. Day by day, he observed just how slowly Carman progressed. He watched as Carman slept most of the day. He observed Rosalie's difficulty feeding Carman, and the baby's failed attempts to play or even crawl around the floor with her. He just wasn't strong enough yet. Joey sat on his sofa, closed his eyes in hopes of shutting out the pain. He felt helpless to care for this kid, his family, or even himself.

Time had stopped for him. His successful boxing career, his big pay checks, and his good times—all on hold because of one misguided, foolish, hard-drinking night with the wrong crowd.

The unknowns and inaction finally got to him. He couldn't sit around the house any longer and wait for something, anything, to happen. In early July, he took the initiative and suggested that his lawyer pay a visit to the DA and see if he could make a deal. It was a bold move.

First, Joey's managers convinced him that he needed to hire a public relations professional to help him stay on the right side of the law and improve his public image. The PR professional's rules were strict: No hanging around with his old cronies. No bars. Be home every night by 10:00 p.m. Perform charity work. After a staged charity function that ended at 8:00 p.m., Joey's managers and the public relations specialist headed out to see a fight. Not Joey, he had to go home. Asked by a reporter who had attended the event how he felt about having to go home early, Joey answered. "It's a good thing. Why, I ain't had a fight with my wife in weeks." His answer was glib but he certainly didn't feel any levity over the situation.

Awaiting a response from DA Dilworth, Joey reflected on his downward spiral and the possible reasons for it. He lamented to his managers, "This all happened because of my son Carman. After I found out that he was retarded, I think that it hit me. You know. I hung around the bars too much. And last year started out so good 'till I found out about Carman. His Down syndrome thing really got me down. Now everything's in turmoil."

Rosalie discovered ways to cope with the instability. Her strength came from within and she endured. She now knew Carman would learn eating, crawling, walking, and everything more slowly than Joseph, but she had no concept just how much slower. She recalled, "I don't think Carman's Down syndrome diagnosis affected me that much. I cried at first, then a mother's instinct took over. For fourteen months, Joseph had colic and screamed all the time. Carman was quiet. He just stayed in the playpen. I felt guilty afterwards. I made that child stay in the pen and the crib. He never even whimpered. In the beginning, he couldn't even suck on a bottle, or roll over, or sit up. It made me feel so guilty that the boy was so good and I just let him sleep."

Talking and toilet training would still be years away.

❋ ❋ ❋

Joey's lawyer returned with the DA's offer. *The deal*—and Joey's later comprehension of it—proved to be two totally different understandings. Joey recalled, "My lawyer comes back from Dilworth's office and tells me, thirty days in jail and I get my license back. Now the DA has me shut down. He took my Pennsylvania boxing licenses and I can't leave Philadelphia." After a short time considering the offer, Joey says, "Let me do the time. I'm going broke."

The DA's offer designated that Joey report to Moyamensing prison. Built in 1835, the castle-like penitentiary was known to be rundown and dirty. Joey balked: "I want to go to Holmesburg prison." Holmesburg was somewhat newer than Moyamensing. A reporter penned the famous line from Dante's *Inferno* at Holmesburg's grand opening in 1896. *Lasciate ogne speranza, voi ch'intrate* ("Abandon all hope, ye who enter here").

The DA readily agreed to send Joey to Holmesburg.

Joey laid down additional stipulations before accepting incarceration. "I want to play on the baseball team and I'm going to jail in my own car. And if I see one reporter outside, I'm not going in." The DA again agreed.

Three days after celebrating his 25th birthday, Joey was driven by a friend to Holmesburg on July 20, 1955. He knocked on the door, the guards answered, and he walked in. "As soon as they closed the door behind me, I realized that I'd done the wrong thing. I overlooked that Dilworth wanted me in prison until November after the election for the Negro vote." It was only July. "That's what burned me up."

When exactly thirty days had expired, Joey asked Rosalie during one of her weekly visits, "When am I getting out?" Like the questions Joey asked about Carman's condition, Rosalie had no answer for her husband.

Joey's understanding of thirty days incarceration was an interpretation of the DA's offer verbalized to Joey by his lawyer. The written and signed deal delineated up to eighteen months. There were still three months, two weeks and five days until Election Day, November 8, 1955.

The Bottom

Incarceration in Holmesburg constituted hard time. There was no comparison between it and the many Federal country-farm, minimum-security correction facilities located nearby in bucolic, rural Pennsylvania. Philadelphia's most notorious criminals were sent to Holmesburg, although the facility is perhaps most infamous for "human guinea pig" testing by the CIA, U.S. Army, Dow Chemical, and Johnson & Johnson. The testing covered a period from 1951 to 1974 and allegedly violated the Nuremberg code and the Hippocratic Oath. It has been reported that everything from radioactive isotopes, LSD, and infectious diseases, to a variety of pharmaceuticals, manufactured by private drug companies, were tested on the inmates. Dr. Albert Kligman, biologist and pioneer dermatologist from the University of Pennsylvania who headed the experiments, stated upon his first visit to Holmesburg, "All I saw before me were acres and acres of skin. It was like a farmer seeing a field for the first time." (1)

Joey Giardello's skin lay among those acreages. Even without volunteering for the experiments, he suffered enormous pain. "Every week the guards would tell me that I'm getting out soon. Then I'd wait. When the guys came back from court, I'd ask them, 'Is my name on the list for court tomorrow?' They'd answer, 'No.' That's why it was hard time for me. I was really hopeful of getting out in thirty."

Weeks crawled into months. "My lawyer said, 'Joey, don't get into any trouble in there. Don't get into any fights.' Well, some of the guys wanted to fight me. I wouldn't fight but I'd show them a few things. I played baseball. That was my sport."

Giardello was asked to testify late September, 1955, during an investigation by the Pennsylvania Boxing Commission looking into boxers with Mafia connections. At the hearing, Joey admitted borrowing $200 from the uncle of one of his co-managers, Anthony Capronigro, also known as Tony "Bananas". Joey testified that he didn't know that Capronigro had a criminal record and didn't know what he did for a living. The day after his testimony the newspapers screamed: "Giardello Linked to the Mob." The warden told Giardello, "You're getting a bad rap." Then hard time became unbearable time when the warden visited Giardello the following day with devastating news.

"Joey, I hate to inform you, but your father died. And I'm sorry, but you're not eligible for a furlough." Giardello recoiled from the news. He loved his dad.

After collecting himself, he asked, "What's that mean, not eligible for a furlough?"

"It means you can't attend his funeral."

Like an AC current, grief and rage alternated powerfully within Joey's body. Air evaporated from his lungs quicker than a punch in the gut from Rocky Marciano. When he could breathe again, Joey grabbed onto the bars. He stared at the warden and waited. The warden's eyes dropped to Joey's hands and watched his knuckles turn white. He instinctively stepped back from the cell.

Before Joey crossed the threshold into rage and tore his cell apart, the warden added, "But let me see what I can do."

That statement had the desired effect. Joey quieted down and began to reminisce: "I loved my father. I remember the first ballgame he ever took me. It was on my eleventh birthday, Dodgers against the Cardinals." Joey sat and buried his head in his hands. "He was a great man." The last remark barely whispered. Tears squirted out of his tightly closed eyes. He muffled the sobs. The warden and those near him grew quiet. Silence is a rarity in prison.

The warden made contact with the right people. Word quickly got back that Joey would be given a furlough.

On Sunday, September 25, 1955, a guard drove Joey to his South Philadelphia home, where they picked up Rosalie, Joseph, and Carman for the hundred-mile trip to Brooklyn. For the evening Joey should have been locked up, but instead, Joey gave the guard a $100 bill and talked him into releasing him to the custody of a cousin, a member of New York's Finest, where he spent the night. The nervous guard slept uneasily at a nearby hotel praying that Giardello would show the next day. He did. The Tilellis attended the Mass and funeral of Joey's beloved father, Joseph Tilelli. The uniformed officer was required to stand next to Joey as he said a prayer over his father's coffin. This caused Joey a great deal of embarrassment. His brother, Bobby, heard him end with a pledge to his deceased father. With teary eyes, Joey leaned over his father and said, "Dad. I'm gonna win you the championship. I promise. And I'm gonna do it as a Tilelli!"

When they returned to Philadelphia later that evening, a tire on the guard's car mysteriously went flat while parked in front of Joey's home and everyone was inside. Joey handed the guard the keys to his new Oldsmobile, still with the dented trunk, and convinced him to go home and return to pick him up in the morning. Joey spent another precious night in freedom. He would later hypothesize: "I don't know if the kids let the air out of that tire or what. They may have thought the cops were bugging us." A broad smile suggested that he undoubtedly knew the answer to the question.

Enlightenment

The mood was somber that night, as Joey reflected on the death of his father, incarceration, ruined boxing career, lost income, and Carman's condition. In exasperation, he asked Rosalie, "What are we gonna do, Rose?" She studied her husband, then made the pronouncement that would dramatically change their lives:

"We're going to stop thinking about ourselves and start thinking about the boy."

Her answer zapped the dark cloud that had enveloped her husband and shocked him back into the reality of what was truly important in their lives—the children. Particularly, the special needs of their Down syndrome boy, little, precious Carman.

Joey bought into Rosalie's forceful argument. From that day forward, no father would do more for the welfare of a child than the notorious "Bad Boy of Boxing"—the former hooligan from South Philly.

(1) Canadian Journal of History, April 2001; "'Human guinea pigs demand justice," H.P. Albarelli Jr., 2008 WorldNetDaily.com

Frank Sinatra and Joey Giardello kept up a running feud to see who could keep the other waiting longer outside his dressing room. A good bet would be that Sinatra won or didn't play for very long.

7

The Journey Upward Begins

"Joey, you're getting out tomorrow!" yelled a guard as he passed Giardello's cell.

"You're crazy! Tomorrow's Armistice Day; there's no court!" replied Joey.

"Mark my word," the guard fired back.

Just as Joey had surmised, three days after the November polls closed that declared District Attorney Richardson Dilworth Philadelphia's newest mayor, Joey was called to court on a Federal holiday and given his discharge. Judge Little from Susquehanna County, over 125 miles north of Philadelphia on the New York state line, was summoned. The judge complained to reporters before the hearing that he had to drive all the way south through heavy snow. There was one last hurdle to jump before Joey's release. The gasoline station owner was awarded a $1,000 judgment. It had to be paid before Joey would be freed, so he yelled to his manager in the courtroom, "Pay the fine! Pay the guy!" Joey added, "If I have to go back in the joint today, I'll really be sick."

Maybe because of his long, scary drive, Judge Little took additional time to lecture the defendant long and hard. "God is good to everybody. If you go back to your church, attend it faithfully, and follow what you learn there, you will have the strength to be the kind of man you can be, and the kind I expect you are going to be. You can live down what has happened in the past, and out of the past you can raise something that you and your friends can be mighty proud of. You can be an outstanding gentleman and you can lead others to where they should go. You have great power to lead young men along the proper path because they have a great deal of respect for you. No matter whether you become champion or not—and I hope someday you may. You will never taste the satisfaction out of anything in this world that you will taste if you use your life to direct others in the right way."

Judge Little lived until 1972. If he followed the news out of Philadelphia over the years, then he may have read or heard whether his long lecture ever had an effect on the middleweight contender.

Restitution for the broken window on the night of the initial arrest might have prevented charges from ever being brought against Giardello in the first place. Joey had to live with that thought and the additional poor decisions that he had made the previous October during the "Riot on Broad Street."

On that quiet Friday of November 11, 1955, Joey walked out of Holmesburg prison after serving four and a half months of a "30-day" sentence. A lone photographer from the *Philadelphia Inquirer* witnessed the release and took Joey's picture with the prison in the background. An entirely different man walked out of Holmesburg that day than had walked in, and it wasn't the incarceration that changed him. It was Rosalie's words and his commitment to honor and to live by them:

We have to stop thinking about ourselves and think about the boy.

The first order of business for doing just that required reinstating his boxing license, climbing into the ring, and quickly earning a few purses. By early January, Joey had jettisoned his managers, Carmen Graziano and Anthony Ferrante, both blacklisted by the Pennsylvania Boxing Commission, and hired former Philadelphia boxer Francis DeVicaris. On January 26, 1956, the PA Boxing Commission reinstated Giardello.

Not only had Joey's household bills been piling up while he was in prison, but he had to cover sizable legal fees and repay the loan to his ex-managers for advancing the $1,000 judgment.

An aide to Dilworth had visited Giardello a few days before his release and informed him that it was unfortunate the DA had been required to pursue the assault charges; and that it was a shame that it resulted in incarceration. He asked Giardello if he was willing to forget everything. The mayor-elect had sought to make sure that Giardello wouldn't cause him any future grief after his release—like a wrongful arrest suit.

Joey agreed.

Immediately after Dilworth's inauguration, Giardello received a beautiful letter from the Mayor stating that he was behind Joey and that he would help him get his license, his career, and life back on track. Dilworth wished him well.

Forever after Joey would bemoan the sad circumstances regarding his jail time with a series of remarks to family, friends, the media, and anyone else who would listen. "I wasn't guilty. I never hit the attendant with my crutch. Dilworth wrecked my life. I was the number one contender. He wrecked me. I had sponsored a kids' baseball team—'Giardello AC.' After prison, the mothers took my name off their jackets. That really hurt. It hurt me." Perhaps a coincidence, or a case of art imitating life, a similar scene takes place in one of the movie *Rocky* sequels. As a South Philly youth, Sylvester Stallone could have witnessed this event as a nine-year old.

Joey asserted his innocence. "Eighty percent of the people around Passaunk and Moore knew the story. They knew I wasn't guilty. They still will tell you that it was a political thing. That bum wanted to be mayor and he become mayor."

Whether with or without Dilworth's help, Joey obtained boxing licenses in the states where he needed them. On February 11, 1956, Joey returned to Trenton, site of his first professional bout for his initial fight after his release from Holmesburg. He posted a win. However, the jail-linked layoff had cost him his number one ranking; now he was designated among the lowly unranked.

Joey didn't care. He was focused on his career, his family, and most of all, on being the very best father for Carman that he could be. Life was not without further problems, though. Joey was released but placed on parole for the balance of his maximum 18-month sentence. That amounted to more than a year of supervised life. His parole officer proved tougher than Sugar Ray Robinson in his prime. He appeared to delight in brutalizing Joey. "He'd come over the house and tell me what I was doing wrong. He'd say that if he ever catches me in a bar—back to jail I go. I told Rose, we gotta get out of here," said Joey. They sold the house and moved to Brooklyn, where one of Joey's brothers had just purchased a house with a six-room apartment on top. Joey and family moved in before his brother did.

It was during this time that Joey jettisoned his co-managers, Carmen Graziano and Tony Ferrante, because the Pennsylvania Boxing Commission found that some of the pair's associates were closely affiliated with or were actual members of the Mafia.

Named was Philadelphia restaurateur Frank Palumbo, who along with Blinky Palermo managed fighter Billy Fox. Jake "Raging Bull" LaMotta admitted that he threw the 1947 fight with Fox at the request of the mob so that he'd get a title shot. Joey and LaMotta were good friends and Joey never faulted LaMotta for what he did, but that he talked about it afterward.

"I was approached by 'the boys' a few times. I never took a dive but I could understand if somebody did. You had your family to protect," Joey explained: He was talking about protecting Rosalie and the kids, not a mob family.

Giardello blamed Blinky Palermo for a loss he suffered when Palermo allegedly bought the judges for his fight against Johnny Saxton in September, 1953. Joey's good buddy, former featherweight champ Willy Pep, reported in his book, *Friday's Heroes:* "One judge had six rounds even. Blinky Palermo was big in Philadelphia where the fight was held. That's a lot of help in your [Saxton's] corner." (2)

From July 1956 through June 1957, Joey racked up 16 straight wins without a loss. Focused? He proved it. He also trained more than ever before and limited his party-time. He no longer required the services of a public relations consultant. His head cleared for perhaps the first time in his life. "I was determined. No more kidding around. I ran, skipped rope, and hit the bags. I had this new manager, Frank Lorenzo, and he kept telling me, one more win, and we go for the championship," recalled Joey. After 17 months he vaulted over all but three middleweight contenders internationally who sought the middleweight division's crown then held by Carmen Basilio.

The Giardellos left Brooklyn and moved to Rosedale in Queens about the same time that New York City Mayor Robert Wagner offered the Brooklyn Dodgers a new baseball park, in, of all places, Queens—a last attempt to keep the team from moving to the West Coast. Dodgers' president, Walter O'Malley, considered the offer an insult. Joey's beloved baseball team departed for Los Angeles. Joey would never forgive O'Malley for this betrayal.

In early May, 1958, Joey flew to San Francisco for a fight. To join him there, Rosalie rode the rails most of the way on the Atchison Topeka & Santa Fe, with Joseph, now six, and four-year-old Carman. "The train ride was wonderful. It took three days and it was luxurious," Rosalie said. Joey extended his West Coast trip and escorted the children down the California coast to Disneyland in Anaheim just south of Los Angeles. The outing with Mickey Mouse also afforded him the opportunity to visit with all his old Dodgers buddies. He heartbrokenly missed one good friend, though—Philadelphia-born Roy Campanella, who had been permanently crippled after an auto accident on the icy streets of New York City a few months earlier. Sadly, "Campy" would never catch a *Los Angeles* Dodgers pitcher.

Joey lost four of his next eight fights. After each loss his manager would say, "You blew it." Joey would answer, "I blew it my foot!"

The Giardellos returned to Philadelphia in 1960 when Joey, finally offered a title bout with NBA middleweight champion Gene Fullmer, needed to move closer to a training facility. He had tired of traveling from Queens into Manhattan each day to train at the world-famous, proudly filthy Stillman's Gym. Once again, this time with two children, they moved back with Rosalie's parents in South Philly.

Joey then took the next step in his personal quest; he joined a number of retarded-children's organizations. Now and for the rest of his life, Joey would work tirelessly for the betterment of disabled and mentally retarded children. He gave his money, his time, and most of all, his heart to the many children whom he'd meet on this new, salubrious journey.

First Title Shot

While the backhoe excavated the foundation for their new home, located in the Philadelphia bedroom community of Cherry Hill, New Jersey, Joey first received word that champion Gene Fullmer had agreed to a fight. "I didn't believe my manager when he told me," Joey admitted.

He flew to Bozeman, Montana, the site Fullmer chose for the championship match. Known as a hard-punching brawler who charged into opponents, sometimes leading with his head, the champ had ordered the smallest ring allowed. The undersized ring would limit Giardello's maneuverability—one of his strongest assets. Smart money bet on the champ to retain his title and little money would accrue to Giardello. He was only offered $25,000 but took the small purse for a chance to win the National Boxing Association crown— the more widely recognized half of the now split middleweight title. The bloody battle lasted the full 15 rounds: a first for Joey. Both men butted heads and were warned by the referee numerous times.

The fight judged a draw; the crown remained with the champion, Gene Fullmer. "Gene was one of the dirtiest fighters around. I butted him. I admit it. I didn't say, 'Excuse me, it was an accident,' like he did. He butted me four or five times," Joey said after the fight. With bitterness in his voice, he added, "I won nine or ten rounds. They just gave it to him, the big shot in Montana."

However, Joey swallowed the decision and moved on with his life and career, something that he probably wouldn't have been able to do as well, if at all, before Rosalie's mandate to "Think about the boy."

(1) NBA, National Boxing Association. The WBA, World Boxing Association, formed in 1962 after the NBA sought to become a universal body. Paul Pender was the World middleweight title holder in 1960 at the time of the Fullmer/Giardello bout.
(2) *Friday's Heroes*, Willy Pep with Robert Saachi, Frederick Fell Publishers, Inc., 1973.

In 1969 Carman is congratulated by his dad and Senator Edward Kennedy for winning a race at a Baltimore, Maryland, regional Special Olympics meet. The win entitled Carman to compete in the Chicago 1970 international games.

8

South Philly to South Jersey

Opened in 1957, the Walt Whitman Bridge, named for perhaps Camden County, New Jersey's most famous resident, hastened the "white flight" as its entrance ramps located on the Pennsylvania side skewered the heart of the Italian South Philly neighborhood.

For the second time, the Giardellos packed up from Rosalie's mom and dad's home and drove over that bridge to take up residence in Cherry Hill, a white, middle-class utopia of the time, and future home of America's first indoor shopping mall east of the Mississippi. Looking similar to the Giradello's custom new tri-level home, track-houses helped swell the population of the town, once horse country and farmlands, from 10,000 in 1950 to triple that number by 1960.

Joey, now aged 32, considered almost an elder inside the ropes, visualized his time as a pugilist nearing an end—his chances for the middleweight championship crown all but out of his reach, according to most experts. Even Joey, for almost fifteen years a top-ranked contender admitted, "I'm near done. I'm too slow. I'm all but washed up."

Rosalie and Joey's two sons, Joseph, now 10, and Carman, now 8, easily adjusted to their new surroundings. Rosalie finally owned that expansive green lawn she'd envied six years earlier during the solemn trip to the hospital for Carman's test results.

Joey spent much of his free time with Carman. He noticed that, as predicted, the boy's mental capacity was greatly diminished compared to Joseph's. But Joey also perceived that while Carman's motor skills were slow to develop, the boy possessed natural athletic ability.

He could catch and throw a ball well. He could run. He was muscular and ran genuinely fast for his age and size. Joey also noted that, as Rosalie had foreseen, Carman caused absolutely no conflict in the home. Rosalie said, "That's how come he turned out to be, we feel, as good as he was, because we never let there be conflict. When my son Joseph got punished for something, Carman got punished for whatever he did wrong. He had *discipline,* they were *very well mannered.* We took them to fights. They had to *sit for hours* at the table when Joey was talking to his managers." Rosalie hit her key points with extra emphasis. "We treated them [both] like normal." Carman's generous smile and easy way made him *the* celebrity in the Tilelli household. Joey Giardello ranked a distant second to this rising star, and Joey couldn't have been more delighted about it.

❋ ❋ ❋

The engraved invitation began:

1789   1961

The Inaugural Ball
To honor the President of the United States and Mrs. Kennedy …

The newly elected President of the United States, John Fitzgerald Kennedy, indeed requested the presence and Mr. and Mrs. Giardello to his Inaugural Ball. This wasn't the typical fund-raising invitation; this invitation to the preeminent of five scheduled balls arrived prepaid.

Joey invited three couples to join his and Rosalie's table. The group took the train from Philadelphia to Washington. They watched part of the Inaugural Parade, but it was biting cold, so they walked to the Goldie Ahearn's restaurant, owned by a fight promoter friend of Joey's. Hotel rooms were, as usual, at a premium during the Inauguration. The group needed to use the restaurant's facilities, especially the bathrooms, where they could all change into their evening wear. Joey climbed into a full-tailed tuxedo and Rosalie slipped on her new ballroom gown. The women of the party wore Arab-like turbans during the day to protect their hair, and were fortunate to have a hairdresser among the group to touch up and puff up as required.

The ball was being held at the National Guard Armory building, where Joey's pal, Frank Sinatra, had performed to the music conducted by Leonard Bernstein the previous night. Ella Fitzgerald, Nat King Cole, Ethel Merman, Gene Kelly, Janet Leigh, and Tony Curtis had joined Sinatra at a typical Hollywood, bash-style show performed for President-elect Kennedy, his family, and entourage. Kennedy had spoken briefly at 1:30 a.m., then hurried off to bed before his big day, when he'd take the oath and officially captain the Ship of State.

The National Guard Armory permitted little room for dancing as the orchestra played continually all evening. It was packed hip to butt, elbow to back, so crowded that Rosalie complained. "I can't even raise my champagne up to drink." But she felt it worth the tiresome wait when the band finally blasted "Hail to the Chief" as the President arrived. "It was so thrilling," added Rosalie.

Naturally, Joey had to get closer to the action. He managed to stand next to President Kennedy, at which time he was presented with one of the official memorial coins, picturing President Kennedy on one side and Vice President Johnson on the other. Joey beamed with satisfaction. Here was "the bum," standing next to the first Catholic President. Next to the President and Jackie stood his sister, Eunice Shriver, who knew all about mental retardation, and cared so much for special-needs children like Joey and Rosalie's beloved Carman. She, a member of the Kennedy clan, would soon call on the President and Joey to help with her grand plans to assist retarded children around the world.

The trip home proved more of a hassle than the trip to Washington. The Giardello party had to change clothes in the railroad station's lavatories before boarding. It was rainy, cold, "Republican weather" as described by a host of the Ball, but few complained. It was an experience of a lifetime for Joey, Rosalie, and their companions. "I didn't even vote for the guy. I voted for Nixon because he was so nice to Carman when we visited the White House to see Eisenhower. But I'll vote for Kennedy next time," said Joey.

Sadly, he would never get the chance to make good on that promise.

The couple's third son, Paul, arrived in September, 1962. When doctors proclaimed the newborn healthy and "normal," Rosalie and Joey were overjoyed. By then, though, they had learned that having a child with Down syndrome wasn't a detriment to their family's happiness. It actually proved an extremely positive experience. In Carman's presence, Rosalie and Joey realized that they had given birth to a human love-generator. He imparted and received more affection from family and friends than they had ever dreamed possible. Until the day he died, Rosalie's father insisted that there was nothing wrong with Carman. If anything, he felt that the rest of humanity was missing an important extra chromosome.

Fortunately, Carman did not exhibit any of the sometimes-severe physical ailments—congenital heart defects and thyroid problems being the most common—that can impede the health of a child born with Down syndrome.

A Second Chance for the Belt

"I don't know exactly how it happened, but I'm told, 'Beat Ray Robinson and you get a shot at the title.'" Joey couldn't believe it. "Ray Robinson would never fight me when he was champ." But this time Robinson was chasing the title. The champ, Nigerian-born Richard Ihetu, who renamed himself Dick Tiger after a friend said that he attacked opponents like a tiger, had announced that he'd fight the winner of a Robinson/Giardello match.

Robinson had been reluctant to take the fight. He told longtime Madison Square Garden matchmaker, Teddy Brenner, "Giardello doesn't like blacks."

"No, that's not true," Brenner assured him. "Giardello has fought all the tough black fighters—Georgie Benton, Spider Webb, Holly Mims, and Bobby Boyd." According to Joey, Brenner also told Robinson that he couldn't get hurt, that Giardello was all washed up. He recommended Robinson take the fight.

He did.

The combatants met on June 24, 1963, at Philadelphia's Convention Hall.

Joey knocked Robinson to the canvas in the fourth round and went on to capture a unanimous decision. Afterward, Joey refrained from demeaning the age-slowed, former champion but instead praised his opponent. "He was a great, great champion." Now Joey hoped Dick Tiger would follow through with his promise.

Robinson could have had a good excuse for losing the Giardello fight—exhaustion. Paranoid of elevators, he had walked to the top floor of the *Philadelphia Inquirer* building the previous day for the weigh-in.

Years later, boxing fans would complain to Giardello that Robinson was old for that fight. Joey always countered. "I was old too." Joey would turn 33 on his next birthday after their fight. Robinson had reached 41 by then.

Dick Tiger, true to his word, set a date for the fight. He would meet Giardello in December, placing his middleweight crown on the line. Tiger even agreed to fight in Atlantic City as Joey still hadn't obtained a license to fight in New York, and Tiger favored Madison Square Garden. The fact that the Giardello team offered more money if the fight took place in New Jersey helped Tiger make the decision. Joey had split with Tiger on their two previous bouts.

Two middleweight champs relax during a friendly game of pool, although Rocky Graziano appears ready to mix it up if Joey makes the shot. Rocky was one of Joey's idols and a lifelong friend.

9

Nearing and Clearing the Top

Carman's formal education began in Cherry Hill, New Jersey's public school system, a dozen years before passage of the Education of the Handicapped Act (EHA) of 1975.

In 1963, neither the public nor the parochial schools in New Jersey provided nor were required to offer special programs for retarded students. But that would change after Camden Diocese's Archbishop Celestine Damiano decided to tackle the special education issue. Joey Giardello jumped first in line to render assistance.

That same year, a Brother from Ireland, Columcille Candon, arrived in Haddonfield, a town adjacent to Cherry Hill, for an extended stay. The purpose of his visit was to raise funds for his order, the Hospitaller Brothers of St. John of God. The Order's roots dated back to 1537 in Granada, Spain, where a homeless, former asylum patient, Juan Cuidad from Portugal, began a mission to help the mentally impaired in need of care and shelter.

Archbishop Damiano suggested to Brother Candon that if he wished to acquire funds in Camden County, he should make plans to give back to the communities from where the money was raised. He offered Brother Candon a suggestion that would solve a monster problem for the Dioceses of Camden, and create a revenue-generating mechanism to also help Brother Candon's Order. The

Archbishop would soon launch two organizations: The House of Charity and St. John of God School.

Joey was ready to assist Archbishop Damiano in any way he could. First, though, he needed to take care of some business that would provide the celebrity to further bolster the Bishop's plans: Secure and win a middleweight championship fight.

❆ ❆ ❆

Word came out of Dick Tiger's camp that he would fight Joey for the middleweight title if the money managers and promoters could work out the deal. It was a big *if*. A number of individuals wanted to make the fight for their own selfish reasons.

Naturally, Joey wanted a second crack at the title. "After fifteen years and a hundred-twenty-nine fights, it would be terrible if I hadn't been the champ," he said.

Tiger's manager, Wilfred "Jersey" Jones, selected Giardello over all the other contenders because he believed that Joey would be the easiest to beat. The Tiger camp considered Georgie Benton but decided that he was too tough. Benton had bested Giardello in 1962.

The image of Joey as a pasta-eating beer guzzler with a lazy training regimen followed him until the day he quit boxing. Never mind that it was unfounded and untrue; one doesn't win 100 career fights when out of shape and unprepared. Perhaps the label stuck as a result of former Philadelphia DA Dilworth's highly quoted sarcastic jabs about Joey, widely reported in the media almost a decade earlier.

Fight trainer Lou Duva was eager to join the big leagues as a promoter. Duva later explained to a reporter how he convinced Giardello to take him on. "Everybody had dumped him. He was down and out until I talked him into letting me promote his shot at the title." Since the boxing commission had rules against a trainer promoting a fight, Duva paired up with Murray Goodman, a known entity around New York boxing. "I sat down with the right people and worked out the right deal," Duva said. "I never sat down with [Frankie] Carbo (the Mafia's underboss of the boxing business), but there were other people I sat down with." (1)

Jersey Jones also met with Duva. "We made the match after I outbid Benton's handlers. They [Dick Tiger's people] didn't know what his [Giardello's] condition was like. But as far as I was concerned, Joey was in excellent condition," Duva said. (2)

Now in better shape than imagined, Joey prepared to build upon his current physical conditioning regimen. In mid-November, he moved his camp to Atlantic City. Not known for his roadwork, he began a new routine at the city's airport. "I ran around Bader Field twice each morning every other day. It was the first time that I really got into it. I figured this was my last hurrah," he said.

Of course he didn't run laps the weekend following November 22, as a paralyzed nation stopped living to watch the burial of President John F. Kennedy. Arizona's great meteor crater in Winslow could not have held all of America's tears.

Joey's public relations people had invited President Kennedy to attend the fight. Joey received a letter in response stating the President's schedule would not permit his attendance, but that he wished him the best. The letter arrived a day after the assassination.

Before the championship fight with Dick Tiger, Joey had an important errand to run. He drove from Atlantic City, where he was training, to the Philadelphia airport. There he personally retrieved his childhood idol, Joe Louis. He escorted the former champ back to an Atlantic City hotel. Joey considered it a magnificent honor just to be in the company of the former heavyweight champion, even for the short drive.

❋ ❋ ❋

Only sixty miles from South Philly, a sold-out Atlantic City Convention Hall overflowed with Giardello supporters. Helped by a nationwide television blackout, attendance swelled to 13,000. Those fans included Joey's four brothers and a busload of friends from Brooklyn.

In an attempt to balance the overwhelming crowd support for Giardello, Tiger brought out his "African witch doctors," who shook a bag of bones and feathers in Joey's direction. Tiger then waited a full fifteen minutes before he entered the ring. Neither tactic appeared to have any effect on Joey. During the long wait he leaned against the ropes, smiled widely, waved to the crowd, and inhaled the constant buzz of fan support.

Tiger had only wasted his own time.

Among those attending the fight were former boxing heavyweight champs, Joe Walcott, Rocky Marciano, and Joey's childhood idol, Joe Louis. Each entered the ring and gave their warmest well-wishes to Joey during the prefight introductions.

Those who witnessed the fight saw a younger-looking, quicker, stronger Joey Giardello than they deemed possible for a battle-weary, 33-year-old boxing warrior. Tiger continually chased the challenger around the ring, but most often his fist met only air where Joey formerly stood. Joey's accurate counterpunches continually smashed into the champ.

At the end of round fourteen, Joey's eyes filled with tears. He knew that victory was not only within his grasp, but just three minutes away. All he needed do for the last round was to jab and dance.

The supportive Joey crowd picked up the volume at the end of the 14th round as Joey skipped to his corner. An old friend in the crowd yelled. "Go get 'em, Chubby!"—a nickname from Joey's Brooklyn grade-school days. Seated ringside just below Joey, Rosalie heard the remark and laughed out loud, breaking the tension that had gripped her from the moment she had entered the arena.

When the bell rang to end the 15th round, Joey's corner men jumped into the ring and hoisted him on their shoulders. They didn't wait for the decision. They knew he had won. The sole arbiter, referee Paul Cavilier, scored the fight 8-5-2 Giardello. The 3-1/2 to 1 underdog was finally the middleweight champion of the world. When it was over, Joey's supporters cheered the ref, letting him know how much they approved of his judgment.

In his dressing room, a dejected Dick Tiger told reporters, "He ran; I fought! I think I fought good enough to retain my title." His manager, Jersey Jones added, "We can't complain about the decision.

It was no robbery. It was the best fight I've seen Giardello make in a helluva long time."

Most fight reporters ringside agreed with Jones. Tiger hadn't thrown the fight away: Giardello had indeed won. He'd reached up and snatched the championship belt. He had earned the right to be called *Champ*.

In addition to losing the crown, a reported mishandling of ticket sales reduced the gate and caused Dick Tiger to complain when he received $78,000 instead of the $100,000 promised. Tiger blamed the mishandling of funds on Jersey Jones. The later discovery of a $10,000 check left for some time after the fight in a friend's safe caused more questions for Jones.

By contrast, one couldn't have found a more contented man in Atlantic City, in New Jersey, or in the entire USA than Joey. "I'm the happiest man in the world!" he exclaimed to anyone within earshot. "Nobody could have beaten me tonight. Not even Rocky Marciano. I was really a master."

Joey held a victory party for 300 at the Ritz Carlton Hotel but a serious problem ensued when close to 1,500 "friends" showed up. There was one guest Joey was happy to see: the Philadelphia Phillies home-run-hitting outfielder, Johnny Callison. Joey idolized Callison and often questioned his heritage. "Johnny, sure you're not Italian? Johnny Calypso?" he'd tease. While said in jest, one can imagine Joey wondering how such a great player could not at least carry some small part of Italian ancestry, like so many of his beloved Dodgers.

Another baseball player, Baltimore Orioles All-Star first baseman, Jimmy Gentile, muscled his way through the crowd to Joey with a present for Rosalie. "He gave my wife a beautiful bracelet engraved with *December 7, 1963* on it," Joey recalled.

"Later we went to the 500 Club after the party and Skinny [Paul D'Amato, alleged longtime front man for the mob. It was the club where Dean Martin and Jerry Lewis got their start and Frank Sinatra entertained regularly] said, 'It's on me, pal. Sit over here!'" The best table in the house awaited the arrival of the champ and his guests.

Joey floated the rest of the way through the evening. "What a feeling. What a night!"

Joey's contingent stayed up until 4:00 a.m., but somehow they and the new middleweight champ managed to attend Mass at 10:00 that morning.

Days after the fight, whenever friends came up to Joey, he'd ask, "Why weren't you at the fight party?" Most had attended. Joey just didn't remember seeing them. One friend responded, "Joey, I was there. We were talking."

"I was on cloud nine. I didn't remember half the people who saw me that night." Joey recalled.

(1) *"Ringmasters,"* Dave Anderson. Robson Books, 1991
(2) *Dick Tiger*, Adeyinka Mankinde. Word Association Publishers, 2004

The world's newest crowned middleweight champion is carried to his dressing room by overjoyed supporters after his 15-round win over Dick Tiger in Atlantic City, December 7, 1963.

10

Championship Reign

During his press conference following the Dick Tiger championship fight, Joey declared, "Now I want to rest a little while and see my kids." He also promised a return bout for the ex-champ. "I'm ninety-nine and nine-tenths sure Tiger'll get a return shot."

This last remark caused Joey immense grief later, when he stalled on setting a date and offering a contract. Jersey Jones failed Tiger once again by not obtaining a return bout clause in the contract before agreeing to fight Joey. But then Jones just may have been supremely confident that Tiger would not be defeated by an *out-of-shape, over-the-hill, washed up* Joey Giardello.

He was probably right; an out-of-shape Joey wouldn't have beaten Tiger. The problem for Jones and Tiger was that Joey trained like never before. He trained like a man who knew that this would be his final shot at the title. He desperately desired the crown, for his family, especially Carman, for the promise that he had made to his deceased father, and for the good that he wanted to do for all special needs children. These children were on his mind when he signed the contract, ran laps around the airport, entered the ring, and lastly, when the bell rang and he knew he'd be crowned champion.

When Joey returned home to Cherry Hill after winning the championship, hand-painted banners covered many lawns. The

"Welcome Home Champ" signs pleased Joey much more than the neighbors might have imagined. When he first arrived in town, he was not sure that those who knew about his past troubles—and most did—were too happy to have a convicted felon and rumored mob-affiliated boxer living next door.

Redemption tasted sweet. Now Joey walked around the neighborhood with his head held just a little higher.

A week after winning the championship, Joey eagerly made the mandatory trip to New York City, where, as a member of the *Ed Sullivan Show* studio audience, he would be recognized by Mr. Sullivan, stand and take the obligatory bow. Carman watched the show on television. For many months thereafter, whenever Carman first saw his father walk in the door, he would intone in his best—and it was very good—Ed Sullivan imitation: "Tonight, on our sh-ooow, the new, world middleweight champion, Jo-ey Gee-har—dello, Gee-har-dello." It never, ever failed to get a huge laugh from the champ and anyone else within earshot.

Joey took four months off before scheduling back-to-back, non-title fights with Juan Carlos "Rocky" Rivero, a hard puncher from Argentina, who once recorded 15 consecutive knockouts in his homeland. His children saw a great deal of their most always absent father during the months after he won the crown. Joseph, 12, Carman, 10, and toddler Paul joined Rosalie in celebrating the family's new togetherness and celebrity.

Paul, unlike Joseph and Carman before him, entered the terrible twos and lived up to that age's turbulent reputation. Rosalie recalled, "Paul was a terror. When we were in Las Vegas for the scheduled Rubin Carter fight, I went through three baby sitters. I finally had to fly my parents out to handle him!" However, Rosalie was now better prepared to handle Paul than when Joseph had turned two and Carman was still an infant. She enjoyed the family more with their father around to share some of the load. (1)

Joey taught Carman how to swim and they played catch nearly every day. Joey loved all of his boys equally, but one couldn't help noticing that a special bond had grown between him and Carman. But then Carman captured nearly everyone with his agreeable, magnetic personality.

Hard work and perseverance had finally begun paying dividends for Joey. He never forgot Rosalie's pronouncement that changed their lives—to think about the boy. He credited this challenge to all the success that followed, and now he planned on enjoying it. As he readied to defend his title, he also made arrangements for a charity bout where he intended to donate all the proceeds toward a new school being built by Archbishop Damiano—the St. John of God School for disabled children that Carman would attend.

But first, there was unfinished business in the ring. Joey won both matches over Rivero, contested in Cleveland during April and May 1964. The first fight, judged a split decision, displeased the crowd, many thinking that Rivero won. The second ended a unanimous win.

The charity "overweight" non-title bout with Gil Diaz was set for April 23. Joey hoped to raise $20,000 for the charities. "Honest to God. I never worked harder for a fight in my life. I'm out selling tickets. Last night I busted into a testimonial for the fire chief. I sold eleven tickets," Joey said.

Joey invited U.S. Senators Robert and Ted Kennedy as well as Sargent Shriver. None was able to attend. About 1,100 paying customers entered the Cherry Hill Arena to watch Joey easily defeat Diaz. According to the promoter, the estimated gate provided less than half of Joey's goal. Joey's net take, about $4,000, was distributed evenly between the Camden County Association for Retarded Children and the Catholic House of Charity. Joey also injured his elbow during the bout, which caused him to cancel a May fight that would have guaranteed him a $17,000 payday plus an all-expense paid trip to Puerto Rico where the contest was scheduled.

Joey attempted to mask his disappointment with levity. "I can't get a break my way. First, I lose four teeth and get five stitches. Now I bang up my elbow. Geez, somebody's gonna have to hold a benefit for me. I'm a wreck."

Tired of waiting back in Nigeria for his promised rematch, Dick Tiger flew to Liverpool, England, where he lived and fought between 1955 and mid-1959. He'd signed for a fight there but it fell through when his opponent sustained an injury while training. A month later, Tiger flew across the pond to New York in hopes of prodding Joey into a rematch and earning a few dollars with tune-up fights. He arrived in June at the very moment that Giardello's handlers announced a title defense against Rubin "Hurricane" Carter set for September in Las Vegas. (1)

Tiger expressed his anger at the timing of the announcement; and, of course, that he wasn't the opponent. He vented his frustration in an article published by *Ring* magazine and denounced Giardello's betrayal:

> Naturally, my one aim now is to regain the world middleweight championship I lost to Joey Giardello on a close decision in Atlantic City last winter.
>
> Whether I will get the chance is something only the future will decide. The prospects at the moment don't appear too encouraging. Giardello doesn't seem too eager to make good on his promise that when he got around to defending the title I would get the first shot at it.
>
> I am keenly disappointed in Giardello's action. In Nigeria we have been led to believe that Americans represent the highest type of sportsmanship, that their words are good as written contracts, and they keep any promises they make. I want to be fair about it, however. Maybe it isn't altogether Joey's fault. He may be badly advised.
>
> I'm hoping Giardello still will be champion after the Carter bout. He's the one I particularly want to meet. I want to prove the Atlantic City result was an accident and it couldn't happen again. (2)

Joey, in no hurry to relinquish the belt, had grand dreams to fulfill first. Over his 15-year career, he always stated that if champion, he'd meet all the No. 1 challengers and put the belt on the line often.

But now, at age 34 and believing in a cause greater than himself, he rethought his official championship reign.

Tough as it was, Joey absorbed the criticism for not living up to his post-Tiger fight exuberant remarks: "I'm gonna be a fighting champion and Tiger is gonna get the first shot. He's got it coming to him." The Giardello team's excuse remained that Tiger disappeared into Africa and that they never heard from him. Tiger complained that his manager, Jersey Jones, never answered his letters, hence the lack of communication between the two camps.

The Giardello advisors may have had second thoughts after the decision to designate the dangerous Rubin Carter, seven years Joey's junior, for a first title defense.

However, Joey believed that he possessed the tactics and skill to defeat "Hurricane" Carter. As for Dick Tiger's complaints, he would just let the Nigerian roar for a little while longer. Deep within, though, Joey always appreciated that Tiger gave him a shot at the title, and forever hence never uttered an unkind word about him.

Tiger would not reciprocate. He spoke like an embittered man: "When I first came to your country, I met many nice people—people who were friendly and kind to me. But if I had met Joey Giardello first, I'm not sure if I would have liked any Americans."

A hard-punching middleweight, Rubin Carter practiced looking mean in the mirror at his Paterson, New Jersey home. The practice wasn't necessary; with his shaved head, Fu Manchu mustache, and physique that could have been chiseled by Michelangelo, he appeared scary enough to most opponents without a scowl. Sporting a 20-4 record, Carter had bested some tough fighters, including George Benton, who had defeated Joey the previous summer.

Carter had won fourteen of his fights by knockouts or technical knockouts; half ended in the first round. Carter came at opponents fast and furious.

The bout, rescheduled from September in Las Vegas to mid-December, took place at Philadelphia's Convention Hall. There Joey summoned all of his ring skills, plus sustained attacks during the last five rounds of the fifteen-round contest in order to assure the win. It proved a unanimous but close decision. A poll of ringside sports writers showed Giardello ahead on fourteen of seventeen cards. The Associated Press reported: *It was like the old matador against the young, dangerous bull.*

During a post-fight conference, both fighters claimed victory but didn't elaborate. Carter said he wouldn't cry over the decision but planned to grow a beard before his next fight. Joey informed the press that his wife was pregnant with their fourth child. Standing alongside her husband, Rosalie blushed when Joey made the announcement.

In Hollywood's version of the bout, produced three decades later and starring Denzel Washington as "Hurricane" Carter, the fight's outcome was shown to be in dispute—a depiction that would cause Joey to battle Universal Studios and its version of Rubin Carter for a second time.

Joey then angered Dick Tiger again. After beating Carter, he suggested that he should fight the winner of an elimination bout between Tiger and Joey Archer.

A holdover from the tragedy-shortened Kennedy administration, Dr. Stafford Warren oversaw President Johnson's mentally retarded children's programs. While in Philadelphia, he learned that middleweight champion, Joey Giardello planned to give the entire proceeds of a non-title bout to the Retarded Children's Association of Camden County and the House of Charity, a Catholic humanitarian organization that also aided children with special needs.

Hearing about this magnanimous offer, Dr. Warren paid a visit to Giardello's South Philly training gym. He listened as Joey explained how he'd dreamed of becoming world champion and then using his celebrity to help Down syndrome children like his son, Carman. Dr. Warren lauded Joey and told the press, "This is the first time an athlete has made a personal contribution such as this, and we think it's wonderful."

The doctor also inspected Joey's busted lip, suffered while clowning around during a sparring match the previous day. "I'm showboating. I don't wear no mouthpiece and the kid belts me. I wind up with stitches in my mouth and I lose three teeth." Standing ringside, Rosalie corrected her husband, "Four teeth!"

Joey informed Dr. Warren that a few weeks previously, he had traveled to Washington and met with Sargent Shriver to discuss the importance of physical training for mentally retarded children. Sargent and Eunice Shriver had been holding informal summer physical education camps at their Maryland home since 1962 for children with intellectual disabilities. Eunice, the sister of John F. Kennedy, was personally touched by their sister Rosemary's developmental disabilities.

While sidelined, Joey attended an April 29 business meeting in Philadelphia, the first of many forums he'd schedule around the country to use his celebrity for furthering the cause of the mentally retarded.

In June, Eunice Shriver requested Joey's presence at a press conference scheduled for her estate in Rockville, Maryland, where she was to unveil a new nationwide program—an initiative designed to emphasize physical fitness for mentally retarded children. The middleweight champion and future boxing Hall of Famer would be joined on the dais by future baseball Hall of Famer Stan Musial, who had just retired from the St. Louis Cardinals, and Cleveland Browns star running back and future Football Hall of Famer, Jim Brown.

Carman, dressed like all the men present, in a well-fitted tweed suit, sat in the rear behind the working press, watching and waiting for his Dad's turn to speak.

Mrs. Eunice Kennedy Shriver, executive vice president of the Joseph P. Kennedy, Jr. Foundation, outlined the new program. Armed with a grant of $600,000 from the Foundation, she stated that the program would provide funds to set up clinics and workshops, give matching grants to communities and schools that developed their own programs, and money for 26 existing camps in 23 states.

Stan Musial, representing the President's Council on Physical Fitness, thanked Eunice and Sargent Shriver for hosting the conference. Musial stated that he looked forward to a productive relationship, staging clinics jointly with the Foundation in cities throughout the country during the school year.

Added Jim Brown, "When I was told that physical fitness and recreation can help the retarded child, I dropped everything. I am here to help. I'm asking Mr. Shriver for an assignment. I want to be on this varsity squad."

Joey stood and spoke briefly from personal experience. "Sports is better for these kids than schools. You gotta give 'em patience, love, and understanding." He added, looking at his son, "It took me a year and a half to teach Carman to hit a ball. Today Carman can hit a ball. I'd take you outside and show you, but it's raining."

Washington Evening Star columnist Morris Siegel captured the presentation with this headline: "Articulate or Not, Giardello Says It Best"

The Joseph P. Kennedy, Jr. Foundation, named for the founder's first-born son, who was killed during WWII, regularly provided funds to hospitals primarily for mental retardation research. This was the first time monies were provided for clinics and recreational programs. Mrs. Shriver estimated that nearly six million retarded citizens resided in the United States in 1964 and many would benefit from these programs.

(1)   The Las Vegas Giardello/Carter fight was called off when the guarantee failed to materialize. It was rescheduled for December in Philadelphia.

(2)   Ring Magazine. December, 1964

The ultimate honor was bestowed upon Giardello in 1993, when he was inducted into the International Boxing Hall of Fame in Canastota, NY.

11

"You the Champ, Dad!"

Two hours remained until Joey Giardello would be called to walk over to Madison Square Garden from his hotel suite. As daylight faded, the neon lights of the Garden gradually brightened along 8ᵗʰ Avenue, luminously declaring it: "Championship Fight Night." Joey was about to place the middleweight belt on the line with the man from whom he took it 22 months earlier—Dick Tiger.

At the moment, he needed to rest. First though, he wanted to get *it* behind him, rather than waiting until later: The Call. He'd promised to talk with his kids before the fight. Normally irritable, anxious, and edgy before stepping into the ring, he was even more so with this call on his mind.

The phone rang; the hotel operator put the call through as he had requested. Joey lunged for it. After a few minutes talking to Joseph, his 13-year-old, Joey asked for Carman. Eleven-year-old Carman meant more to Joey than all the titles, belts, awards, and honors he could accumulate. "Hey, Carman," the champ said.

"Hi, Daddy," said Carman. The boy hesitated then added. "Come home."

"I got to fight first."

"Don't fight first. Come home first. I said a prayer for you."

Joey took a deep breath. "I might lose."

"You the champ, Daddy. You never lose."

After his goodbye, Joey stretched out on the bed. It was tough, but he pushed thoughts of his children out of the way. He closed his eyes. He envisioned how Tiger would come at him. He watched himself avoid the charge, and then turn the attack to his advantage with counter punches—especially the lethal left hook. He moved through this process for all fifteen rounds.

※ ※ ※

The clock in Joey's head told him the fourteenth round would be over in five seconds. He connected with a lead right hand to Tiger's head at the bell. Needing a break for his wobbly 35-year-old legs, Joey flopped on the stool as soon as the trainer thrust it inside the ring.

After cut man Adolph Ritacco finished his work on Joey's bruised eyes and cheek, and he quickly rinsed his mouth, the Champ looked down at *New York Post* writer Al Buck and asked, "How is it?"

Buck raised his shoulders. "You're behind."

Indeed the champ was behind. His corner told him after the twelfth round, "Take these last three rounds and we win." The corner was wrong; Buck was right. In the end, the official score cards read:

      Judge Tony Castellano   8 – 6 – 1 Tiger
      Referee Johnny LoBianco   9 – 5 – 1 Tiger
      Judge Al Berl   10 – 5 – 0 Tiger

For the second time, Dick Tiger of Nigeria had become the new WBA and WBC Middleweight Champion. His nation would celebrate, while another celebration started immediately in Tiger's dressing room. Fellow Nigerians dressed in flowery *agbada* gowns, and highly colored *fila* hats, danced to the beat of Tiger's resident drummer, Olatunji, whose wooden drum could be heard throughout the arena.

※ ※ ※

"He didn't hurt me."

The four words, croaked softly rather than spoken, came from the man who, from now on, would be addressed as the former champion. He hadn't yet changed from his black satin trunks, boxing shoes and one of his eight-ounce gloves. His trainer wrestled with the laces of the second glove as Joey talked. A sweat-soaked towel hung loosely over a shoulder. His robe lay tossed on a chair.

Almost all of those packed into dressing room #28 at Madison Square Garden, who were close enough to view his body, might have disagreed.

Welts colored crimson to deep purple swelled beneath each eye. A gash high over his right brow no longer bled, but drew one's attention. The random blotches on his arms and shoulders offered perfect examples for first-year medical students of burst capillaries coagulating. Soon those wounds would be covered by a long-sleeved shirt. His face would remain bare for all to see, sans the near-opaque sunglasses held at the ready by his trainer. Sweat dripped slowly from an uneven band of dark curls plastered to his forehead.

Melvin Krulewitch, chairman of the New York State Athletic Commission, made his way to the front and reached out to shake hands. "A marvelous display of courage," he said. Joey accepted the gesture with an almost imperceptible nod as he reached out his still-gloved right hand. Concluding the ceremonial requirement, Krulewitch hurried away from the ex-champ and departed the quiet room for the festive winner's dressing room.

Rosalie pushed forward next and carefully kissed her husband on the corner of his uncut but slightly swollen bottom lip.

The kiss defeated Joey's inner struggle between maintaining composure and losing it. He lost it. Rosalie grabbed her husband by the shoulders and turned him away from his manager, trainer, cut man, promoter, friends, relatives, and press mob, all of whom were squeezed into the dressing room. She guided him away as tears flowed down his bruised cheeks.

Consoled for a few moments, Joey walked back, faced the reporters, and explained. "I don't have a tear for the title. Retirement don't mean nothing. It's just my son. I hurt my children."

He was referring to his two boys, Joseph and Carman, who had watched the fight from their New Jersey home.

Close to tears again, Joey walked to the back, where a phone sat on an uncluttered desk. The press mob waited again, talking in low voices, trying to overhear the ex-champ as he talked on the phone. Once again, Joey spoke to the eldest son first, then to Carman.

"Daddy's no longer the champ," said Joey.

Joey shared the earpiece with Rosalie. Carman's small voice responded, "Daddy, you always the champ."

Joey said goodbye, hung up, and wiped the tears from his eyes with the soggy towel. Rosalie handed him a handkerchief. He blew his tender nose, collected himself again, and walked back toward the mob. Time to handle the tough interview he knew would be coming, leeches after the blood of a man who had just lost his championship crown. Each reporter searched for tomorrow's big, bold headline quote to go along with the picture of the beaten brawler. Rosalie gave them one:

"Giardello's Wife Tosses In The Towel"
New York Post, Friday, October 22. 1965

Carman Tilelli and unidentified classmate at St. John of God School review announcement poster with old-time boxers and bishop Guilfoyle for charity bouts scheduled for the Cherry Hill arena, Cherry Hill, New Jersey in 1969.

12

The Father, Son, and Holy School

Perhaps no other educational endeavor launched with a more inauspicious start than St. John of God School of Haddonfield, New Jersey. While the entire nation, most acutely the Irish and Catholic communities, still mourned the loss of President Kennedy, the school's collective resources in late November, 1963, included one cheerless, Irish Brother from the Order of Hospitaller, one rented room, no students, and no revenue.

Initially, Brother Columcille Candon, "Colm" as he liked to be called, opened a shop in the commercial district of the picturesque, historic town. There he sold goods made in Ireland and arranged charter trips to Europe in order to generate funds. Initially the Order wanted to raise money for a new mission in Korea, but Archbishop Damiano approached him with a better idea—help him start a school for special-needs children.

It was a request that would be hard for Brother Colm to ignore, given his Order's modern day primary mission that, in part, states: " Our Mission is to assist people who have disabilities to develop their skills to the fullest potential with *caring* and *compassion,* and to honor the dignity of each individual we encounter."

The Hospitaller Order of St. John of God began around 1545 with even less possibility for success than the school Brother Colm had been asked to help establish.

The Order's founder, John Cuidad, was born in a small Portuguese town around 1495. He left at age eight to explore Europe and North Africa. At about age 40 he settled in Granada, Spain, where he experienced a religious conversion that caused a lengthy stay in a psychiatric hospital. There he witnessed the inhumane treatment of the poor and disabled. Once released, John developed what can be seen as the principals for the treatment of the disabled today. He attracted a small following, which gave birth to the Order that today serves the poor, the sick, the dying, and the disabled in 50 countries around the world. John Cuidad, a Catholic Brother, died in 1550 and was canonized in 1690.

With the substantial backing of Archbishop Damiano, and unknown at the time to the Archbishop or Brother Colm, the idea of a school would soon become the beneficiary of the significant fund-raising efforts of a former middleweight champion.

On December 7, 1965, two years to the day that Joey out-pointed Dick Tiger for the World Middleweight Title, Brother Colm greeted the arrival of four additional Order of Hospitaller Brothers: Thaddeus, Eunan, Canice, and Cornelius. Reverend Father Damien joined the group at the request of Archbishop Damiano, with the specific goal to open a school for children with developmental disabilities.

The Brothers were given an old convent for use as their first school. It was soon filled with seven special needs students. Two lay teachers and a sixth Brother, Brother Raymond Keane from the Order's Rhodesia (now Zimbabwe) mission, were added in 1967 to temporarily complete the staffing. The student population grew to sixteen, ranging in ages from five to fourteen. The basic curriculum focused on reading, writing, and arithmetic. In addition, the instructors placed special emphasis on social skills. The school's charter faculty, the "Order of Hospitaller Magnificent Seven," was completed with the arrival of Brother Sebastian Hyland.

While financial records have not survived, a conservative estimate would suggest that Joey contributed approximately $2,000 (over $13,000 in 2009 dollars) from his Diaz non-title bout to the House of Charity. It is not known how much Archbishop Damiano earmarked for St. John of God School, but construction of a new building commenced shortly thereafter some ten miles away in Westville Grove, New Jersey.

Construction moved fairly quickly on the new facility. St. John of God, Archbishop Damiano School, opened its doors on September 11, 1968, to students. Enrollment at the Westville Grove facility reached 34 and the building expanded to eight classrooms. A cafeteria and an auditorium/gymnasium were later added.

A Parents and Friends Association formed in order to further grow the dream that the families of these special needs children harbored for years, and then watched as it transformed into a reality. The parents became "volunteers" and held many fundraisers.

From her cafeteria report, Mrs. Inez Devan recalled, "The first day of school we served vegetable soup. Milk was purchased and several mothers brought juice. The mothers were called to come in the kitchen and help ... the dishes had to be done by hand." She also noted that the Trenton China Company donated a set of china for 102 persons and the Bond Baking Company supplied the first week's bread. Shortly afterward the school qualified for the Federal Lunch Program and it began serving Type "A" lunches. (1)

Joey and Rosalie heard about St. John of God School through their pastor at Queen of Heaven Church in Cherry Hill. They removed Carman from the public school system and enrolled him. "Carman was fifteen when he went over there. The School had a bus and they got him every morning and took him home every night," remembered Joey.

Rosalie recalled her duties after Carman began attending. "We parents had to get involved. I went on the bus with Carman a couple of times a week and helped out. We knew all the other parents. The students went to Washington on school trips. They were involved with the Boy Scouts. That's when Carman joined the scouts."

Joey added. "They were very good to him. That school did a lot for him. I tried to make money for the school. I got them involved with the Special Olympics."

As had many boxers before him, Joey retired after losing the championship, only to return to the ring and do battle four more times. Finally, on November 6, 1967, Joey Giardello won his very last fight, hung up his gloves, and finally took back his given name, Carmine Orlando Tilelli. While the 37-year-old boxer left the fight game, he used his alias and fame for many years to raise money for his favorite charities: the newly formed Special Olympics and St. John of God School.

By lending his name and energy to philanthropic causes, Joey began to experience a level of happiness he'd never known before. Better yet, Carman was now enrolled at St. John of God, and soon Joey would involve Carman and St. John of God School with one of the greatest programs for special needs individuals ever created— the Special Olympics.

During St. John of God's 40th anniversary in 2005, its mission statement, in part, noted: "St. John of God Community Services is a non-profit, non sectarian agency serving individuals with and without disabilities."

By the year 2009, St. John of God School operated two major facilities and served over 200 residences of southern New Jersey in the areas of special education, vocational and habilitative services, including: early intervention, preschool, elementary education, secondary education, clinic services, vocational rehabilitation/adult services, therapeutic recreation, day care, and nursery school.

(1) From "The Orchard," St. John of God Community Services, Volume 1. Renegade Publishing, 1997

Eunice Kennedy Shriver accompanies Joey Giardello on one of his many road trips to emphasize physical training for mentally disabled children.

13

Born in Chicago and Changed the World

Roman orator, statesman, and historian Tacitus first pronounced, "Success has many fathers, but failure is an orphan." That adage might apply to the etiology of the Special Olympics if altered: "Success has many mothers." Simultaneous events in a Chicago park and on a suburban, Maryland lawn ushered forth a movement that actually did change the world. Beginning in the early 1960s, President John F. Kennedy's sister, Eunice Kennedy Shriver, opened her heart and her estate to special needs children for a place to play and learn sports together. She inaugurated "Camp Shriver," a day camp where as many as 100 mentally disabled youngsters ran, swam, played soccer, and rode horses each summer.

Meanwhile, on the south side of Chicago, a twenty-year-old park service physical education instructor, Anne McGlone, volunteered to begin teaching special needs children at the West Pullman Park facility. "At first it was difficult just to get the parents to bring their kids to the park. In 1960 these children were rarely seen in public. Parents were afraid that they would be ridiculed or taunted," said McGlone.

The idea was presented to the parents that their children would be given a chance to play and enjoy sports with other kids like their own. The parents' protective resistance diminished and some began bringing their young children to the park. However, McGlone's training techniques required radical refinement. "I blew the whistle and asked the children to line up on the blue line. Surprisingly, they continued running around. Then I realized that some or most of them didn't know their colors and didn't know what a line was," she explained. "That occurrence told me where I had to begin."

She met the challenge. Training of special needs children was initiated at nine parks in addition to the West Pullman facility where McGlone blew her whistle.

In 1965, for the first time, the Joseph P. Kennedy, Jr. Foundation provided money to entities other than research facilities. Joey had attended the meeting, along with Stan Musial and Jim Brown, where Eunice Shriver announced a Foundation endowment totaling $600,000, earmarked for physical-education training for children with special needs. The Chicago Park District received a grant of $10,000. Some of these funds reached Anne McGlone. A few years into the program of working with mentally disabled children, two Park District officers, President Bill McFetridge and Vice President Daniel Shannon, on a routine inspection tour, visited McGlone's West Pullman Park and observed the children.

Both were visibly moved and surprised at the level of achievement these children displayed. Near tears, they asked McGlone how many children were in the program. "There's a hundred at my park, probably fifty, forty or more at each of the other nine parks; maybe a thousand all told," she answered. They then asked how many more children like this might be in Chicago. While McGlone didn't know the answer, she suggested that they hold a Chicago track meet and invite the entire city's mentally disabled children to attend. They liked the idea and invited her downtown to explore the possibility of staging such an event.

McGlone's suggestion would ultimately lead to a worldwide movement. This spark of an idea in Chicago ignited a flame in Maryland that launched the International Special Olympics.

When the time came to actually put plans in motion to hold the competition, McGlone contacted Dr. William Freeberg of Southern

Illinois University and asked if he'd consult on the project. In addition to heading SIU's Outdoor Education Program, Dr. Freeberg oversaw "Little Grassy," a day camp for mentally disabled children. "Little Grassy" was the first university-affiliated residential camp for people with disabilities.

It was Dr. Freeberg who had lectured McGlone and nine other Chicago Park District instructors before they began their pilot programs. When McGlone contacted him, Dr. Freeberg accepted the challenge and immediately suggested that she write the Kennedy Foundation to request funds for the city-wide track meet.

Together they wrote a proposal and sent it off to the Kennedy Foundation. Though McGlone had attended Dr. Freeberg's lecture, they hadn't really met, nor was she aware that he had been executive director of the Kennedy Foundation in the early 1960s.

A few weeks after sending the proposal, McGlone flew to Washington and met with Mrs. Shriver to pitch her idea first-hand. Quickly, the plan was approved by the Kennedy Foundation Board of Directors. The stars had aligned and the Chicago Park District would hold its meet.

However, the Kennedy Foundation had a colossal stipulation: that the event be expanded to include the entire United States and Canada. Unperturbed by the request, Anne McGlone, now Mrs. Anne Burke, and the Chicago Park District began implementing their plan. Dr. Freeberg's first action was to suggest that they should request additional funds from the Kennedy Foundation for the now international event. The Foundation provided $25,000.

The date was set: July 20, 1968. Preparations began in earnest. Since the Park District had hosted over 2,000 athletes from around the world for the 3rd Pan American Games held at Soldier Field in 1959, the organization was well prepared, ready and eager to host the first Special Olympics. Mayor Richard J. Daley accepted the challenge to hold the Pan American Games when Cleveland withdrew as the host city. Mayor Daley, a staunch supporter of presidential candidate John Kennedy in 1959, was happy to assist the late President's sister, Eunice, in launching the Special Olympics movement.

Eunice Shriver also got busy. One of the first calls she made was to Joey Giardello. She asked if he would be available in July to attend the first-ever Special Olympics as a VIP coach. Joey was honored; he immediately confirmed, and asked if there was any more that he could do to help. Eunice assured him that lending his name and attending as a coach was all she needed of him.

On that third Saturday in July, the Chicago sky proved sunny, clear, and dry. The temperature was perfect for tee shirts and racing shorts. After a "Breakfast of Champions," the athletes were driven from the Olympic Village, the LaSalle Hotel, directly to Soldier Field, home of the Chicago Bears. At the players' entrance, the athletes departed the busses, each child filled with excitement and nervousness, anxious for the competition to begin.

The opening ceremony, which mirrored the Olympic Games, began with the march of the athletes. As the athletes entered Soldier Field, Chicago mayor Richard J. Daley leaned over to Mrs. Shriver and said: "Eunice, the world will never be the same again." His words would prove prophetic.

Next, the honorary coaches were introduced. Their names and accomplishments blasted over loud speakers throughout the arena. The announcements bounced off empty seats then reverberated onto the field:

"FORMER MIDDLEWEIGHT CHAMPION
OF THE WORLD,
JOEY GIARDELLO!"

Upon hearing his name, Joey broke into his least favorite training regimen by energetically jogging from under the VIP seating area to the infield. He joined the first VIP coach announced, 1955 Heisman Trophy winner, Howard "Hopalong" Cassady, who awaited Joey's arrival on the field. Next came Paul Hornung, one of the Green Bay Packer greats and 1956 Heisman Trophy winner. Following Hornung were Rafer Johnson, 1960 Olympic gold medal decathlon champion; Congressman Bob Mathias, two-time Olympic decathlon champion in 1948 and 1952; and the Chief Coach, Apollo 8 (and future Apollo 13) astronaut James Lovell, chairman of the President's Council on

Physical Fitness. Lovell, of course, would be the only coach to leave earth five months hence and circle the moon on that memorable, 1968 Christmas Eve.

The applause that followed each introduction was long and loud. The flags of the United States and Canada were raised, anthems played, the torch lit, and the Special Olympics flag unfurled. Then Mrs. Shriver delivered these opening remarks:

"In ancient Rome, the gladiators entered the arena with these words:

'Let me win, but if I cannot win,
let me be brave in the attempt.'

"Today, all of you young athletes are in the arena. Many of you will win; but even more important, I know you will bring credit to your parents and your country. Let us begin the Olympics."

Beside the special coaches, collegiate and professional athletes from numerous sports made an appearance, including Johnny Lattner, Rocky Blier, Jim Mello, and Ziggy Czarboski. These men were joined by the entire Notre Dame football team, and many members of the Chicago Bulls, who provided demonstrations and helped coach the competitors throughout the meet. The children reveled with pure joy in the attention and instruction shown them by these famous athletes.

In addition to the track and field events, the Chicago Park District built a swimming pool and a Teflon rink so a Stan Mikita-led Chicago "Blackhawk" team could face off against a George Armstrong-coached Toronto "Maple Leaf" team in "ice" hockey.

The first games hosted 1,000 athletes from the United States and Canada, but with the exception of the families, no one sat in the stands. That would change for subsequent Special Olympics.

At the end of the day's competition, Mrs. Shriver declared the games an overwhelming success. She announced funding for five regional meets the following year, along with the second Special Olympics Games, set for 1970, to be held at Chicago's Soldier Field. Mrs. Shriver hosted the games with remarkable composure given the fact that her brother, presidential candidate Senator Robert Kennedy, had been assassinated in California a mere 45 days earlier.

No official sponsors came forward for the first Special Olympics, nor did it gain much press coverage. Anne Burke remembered how difficult it was for the first games. "We could not get endorsements because they said that we were putting these children on display. We proceeded anyway because we knew that we were right. Afterward, people from Health Education and Welfare came up to us and said. 'It was wonderful.'" She added, "One goal was public awareness and education. Even the parents of these kids didn't know what, if anything, they could do. The games showed that while they might not be able to hit the home runs, at least, they could hit singles."

Burke recalled President John F. Kennedy's resolve to help the mentally disabled: "Although children may be the victims of fate, they will not be the victim of our neglect."

Three days after the first games, Burke received a letter from the Joseph P. Kennedy, Jr. Foundation. It read:

July 23, 1968

Dear Anne:

When the history of the Chicago Special Olympics is written, there will have to be a special chapter to recount the contributions of Anne Burke. You should feel very proud that your dedicated work with retarded children in Chicago has culminated in an event of such far reaching importance.

We all owe you a debt of gratitude, but I know that what means most to you [is] that the [Special] Olympics will continue and that children all over the country will benefit from your idea.

My warmest personal thanks,

Sincerely,
Eunice Kennedy Shriver

Following law school and private practice, Anne Burke received an appointment in 1987 to the Illinois judicial system. She was first appointed by the Illinois Supreme Court, then elected to the Appellate Court in 1996. In 2008, she was elected a member of the state's highest court, the Illinois Supreme Court.

No longer an official of the Special Olympics, Justice Burke traveled to Shanghai, China, in 2008 for the 12th Summer Games. She sat in the stands along with 80,000 others to watch 8,000 young athletes from 175 countries compete. Afterward, Justice Burke observed, "The most important aspect of this [the Special Olympics holding games in China] was that a Third World country, where these children, ten years ago, would not have been born, were celebrating people with disabilities."

She also noted that for the first time, the Special Olympics, in their 12th Summer Games' official program book, had recognized her contributions to the movement during this, the organization's 40th anniversary year.

Former heavyweight champ, "Smok'n" Joe Frazier and former middleweight champ, Joey Giardello, both local Philadelphia heroes, pictured here with an unidentified boxing executive.

14

"Night of Champions"—for the Love of Joey

Many celebrities stage phenomenal events on behalf of their favorite charities. Singers, actors, actresses, athletes from all sports, and even good-hearted politicians pitch in more often than one might expect. Some make unpublicized appearances where only the individual knows, and experiences the joy of giving without thought of recognition. But it would be hard to find a more caring, loving group of celebrities than professional fighters from the Golden Age of Boxing. When asked about this observation in 2008, the popular fighter Chico Vejar, a good friend of Joey Giardello, downplayed the idea. "Na. Many people do many things that you're never aware of. Boxers of my era just did their share."

Despite Chico's lukewarm response, Joey and his pals went way beyond "their share" when Joey put out the call to support his favorite charities: St. John of God School for retarded children and the Special Olympics.

In 1969, Joey proffered an idea to stage boxing exhibitions for charity. He placed calls to his former rivals in the ring—including some still harboring old grudges—and they responded with the eagerness of a movie starlet drawn to a spotlight, not once but twice. They knew no appearance fees were attached to the engagement; furthermore, they had to cover their own expenses. It didn't matter. They came willingly, not just to support the charity, but to show their love and respect for Joey, and to salute him for the remarkable way in which he was raising Carman.

The first exhibition was held on October 23, 1969, in Joey's hometown at the Cherry Hill Arena. The facility was best known as home ice for the Eastern Hockey League team, the Jersey Devils. (1)

The first bout featured a pair of marquee names, Jake LaMotta against Rocky Graziano. The two had never fought during their competitive years, but they happily laced up the gloves and mixed it up for Joey and Carman. It was common for Italian contenders of their era to avoid fighting one another.

The next battlers on the card were just the opposite. Featherweight champions Willie Pep and Sandy Saddler had fought each other four times. Sandy took three out of four bouts, including their September, 1951, fight that was so brutal the New York Athletic Commission suspended both men for a time afterward. Their exhibition fight for Joey was not a bloody brawl but Willie chose not to show up Sandy, as he knew his opponent from Harlem wouldn't take any insult lightly. Sandy would go at it for real if Willie gave him any excuse, and Pep wanted no part of an enraged Sandy Saddler, even at age 43. "I don't try to show him up in an exhibition. With a guy like Sandy you don't fool around because he's a very serious guy and he keeps in shape," remembered Pep. (2)

Middleweight Chico Vejar took on Ernie "The Rock" Durando. Joey's win over Durando in 1951 launched him into Top 10 contending status in his division.

The last fight featured Joey and "Irish" Billy Graham. Not only had Joey beaten Graham in their first fight, but he beat him for a second time in court. The New York Supreme Court upheld the win that was taken from Joey by a New York State Athletic Commissioner who changed a judge's card after the fight. Despite the bitterness surrounding the fight and its aftermath, Graham came to Joey's charity events.

No fight is complete without the ring announcer, and once again, Joey strong-armed the very best to intone the fighters' names, weight (with some trepidation), and color trunks. He brought in the incomparable voice of Madison Square Garden for much of the 1950s and 60s—Johnny Addie.

There was more. As though a fight card already full of past featherweight and middleweight champions wasn't enough to bring out the fans, Joey succeeded in talking former heavyweight title holders Jack Dempsey, "Jersey" Joe Walcott, and Jim "Cinderella Man" Braddock to referee the bouts.

A local sports reporter captured the essence of that evening's matches and the true sentiments of this "over-the-hill gang's" gathering:

> There was more lard than muscle, more 'ham' than skill, more fun than brutality on the card. But the show was worth whatever you paid to get in because these guys who can no longer fight like the kids they used to be have not lost the hearts that made them what they were.
>
> Joey's friends came to Cherry Hill last night do a favor for the man and his son … and the sons and daughters of many others they do not know and will never know.
>
> Joey has friends he can count on. Friends who will do Joey a favor just because he's Joey and not because there is anything that he can do for them … except, maybe return the warm respect they have for him.
>
> Chico Vejar, the erudite spokesman for the fighters, called Joey to the ring late in the show and the crowd responded with a standing ovation which made the one-time champion choke with emotion.
>
> The applause was not for Joey Giardello the middleweight champion but for Joey Giardello, father. (3)

About 1,500 fans showed up for the exhibition in a facility that seated 7,000. The event had raised $10,000 for St. John of God School. Joey was disappointed. "I hoped to raise $30,000. That was my goal." More determined than ever to raise an even greater sum, Joey immediately began planning for an exhibition to be held at the Spectrum, a 20,000-seat arena in South Philly, which served as home to the Philadelphia Flyers hockey and 76ers basketball teams until 1996.

Joey had retired from boxing, but that didn't take the fight out of the man, especially when it came to generating dollars for special needs children like his beloved Carman. St. John of God School and the Special Olympics had been blessed with their very own, and extremely determined, fund-raising angel.

(1) The Eastern Hockey League New Jersey Devils was not the antecedent of the team of the same name now playing in the National Hockey League.
(2) *Friday's Heroes,* Willie Pep. Frederick Fell Publishers, 1973
(3) Bob Wright, *Camden Courier Post,* October, 1969

All dressed up for the Captain's Dinner. Joey introduces Carman to the Carnival Cruise Line captain during Carman's first cruise.

Pop singer and television host of a mid-fifties variety show, Perry Como, autographed his photo with Joey and Carman.

15

Three Hundred Yards

In 1969 Joey took Carman to the Regional Games held in Baltimore, Maryland. There Carman ran and won a medal to qualify for the following year's International Special Olympics Games. Joey introduced Carman to Senator Edward Kennedy, Eunice's younger brother, who hosted the event. To Carman it seemed like a lifetime, but finally mid-1970 arrived.

On an overcast day in the overheated steam room that defined another Chicago August, the former middleweight champ knelt down beside the cinder oval surrounding the grassy Soldier Field gridiron. His weary, 40-year-old legs creaked as he lowered himself. Lined up beside the faded 20-yard line marker, he assessed the competition and checked for the direction of the prevailing wind. Sweat ran in shoulder-width bands under both his arms and soaked the silk shirt that clung tightly to his chest. He wore the Philadelphia Phillies baseball cap that Johnny Callison, the club's popular home-run-hitting outfielder, had given him.

Joey placed a hand on his 16-year-old son's shoulder and locked his eyes onto Carman's. "Now listen to me! This is a long race. Three hundred yards. Okay?"

Carman nodded, but his father wasn't sure he understood.

The champ paused. Carman turned his head and leaned his ear closer to his father's mouth. He stood rigid, waiting for him to speak again.

"Here's what I want you to do." The champ spoke slowly, willing his son to understand. "When you go around the track, I want you to run second, right?"

The boy's head bobbed and he looked back at his father. This time the champ saw recognition in his son's big, wide-set, bright green eyes. "Good. Now stay second until you see me. I'll be standing right here. Understand?"

"Okaydad." Spoken in a low monotone, the words merged together. The champ was accustomed to his son's unorthodox manner of speech.

"Now, when you pass me, go for it. Go for the lead and run as fast as you can. Got that?"

His son nodded once more. "Yeah, I run fast when I see you."

The champ tightened his grip on the shoulder, "No, no. When you run past me, here."

"Okay—when I pass you," Carman repeated.

"Right."

The champ struggled to his feet and tugged up his son's white racing shorts. He patted Carman's shoulder, and with both hands, gently guided him toward the starting line, where nine other anxious competitors had already assembled.

Carman grinned and wrapped his arms around himself. He seemed to understand that he knew something none of the other runners did: How to pace himself on this hot afternoon. He trotted away, then looked back, and waved at his dad. He stumbled and smiled even more widely, his eyes still fixed on his dad.

The champ smiled, shook his head, and laughed. Then he closed his eyes in reproof and waved him on. He watched Carman turn his attention to an official, who led the boy into the middle of the line. The champ offered a quiet prayer: "Dear God, thank you. Thank you for this blessing."

The starter's gun went off. The champ, who had been looking heavenward, flinched. He turned quickly to inspect the runners.

Carman jockeyed into position a stride behind the leader and stayed there. Halfway around the track, another boy challenged for the lead and took it. Carman, now running third, pushed past the former pacesetter to regain second. As the field made its final turn, Carman's eyes met his father's well before he reached him.

The champ's body tensed. "Steady, Carman," he murmured. "Not yet. Wait. Wait."

The boy held back until he reached even with his dad, then burst for the lead. With ample reserve, he easily passed the tiring leader.

Carman won by five yards.

The champ leaped up. "Yes!" His scream filled the air. Poised to run toward his son, he stopped, bowed his head, and crossed himself. "Dear Lord, thank you. This is the greatest moment ... better than the title. Amen."

He blessed himself again and hurried to Carman, picked him off the ground, and swung him around. "You won! You won!"

Carman held his ever-present smile. "You—you crying, Dad?"

The champ put his boy down and rubbed his eyes on his sleeve. "Nawwwh. Wind blew dirt in my eye."

Carman accepted the excuse and spun around in a tight circle until he was dizzy. Then he staggered and fell, laughing all the while. The champ bent over to help him up, but Carman pulled him down and the champ faked a fall and rolled over on the turf beside him. Carman gulped air and tried to catch his breath as he continued to laugh. For a minute, the champ feared that his boy might convulse, but Carman gained control of his breathing and excitement. The champ stared at his red-faced, ever-smiling, Down syndrome son. "Carman, you make me so proud to be your father."

All nine runners walked over with their parents to congratulate Carman, who stood up to meet them. The champ stayed on the ground and watched. God had been good to him—could it get any better?

Later that afternoon, the former middleweight champion stood across from the winner's podium. He watched Eunice Kennedy Shriver place a gold medal over his son's head.

There was no dust blowing, but the champ's eyes glazed over

again.

Mrs. Shriver recognized Joey in the crowd of parents. She knew Joey had met with her husband, Sargent Shriver, three years earlier and had impressed upon him the importance of sports in the early development of children afflicted with Down syndrome. Joey was present at the press conference when she announced that the Kennedy Foundation would fund physical education programs for the mentally retarded nationwide. He attended the first Special Olympic Games two years earlier as a VIP coach. And now, here he was again, a VIP coach and a parent, who had just watched his son compete in the second Special Olympic games. She motioned for Joey to join her in front of the stands and asked if he'd please address the crowd. He stepped forward and stood next to her. She reached out and took his hand for a moment. Joey turned to face the hundred-plus proud parents who waited for him to speak.

Joey opened his mouth. Before any words came, his shoulders rose up once, twice, three times. He closed his mouth and attempted to smile, but his mouth turned downward. The mind that had maintained complete control over a professional-boxing champion's finely-tuned body for seventeen years lost the battle to help the father sustain his composure. Tears overflowed the puffy banks of his bottom eyelids. He squinted, squeezing out even more moisture. He didn't look at Mrs. Shriver, but turned, and walked away.

Mrs. Shriver smiled, and with a slight nod and a shrug, acknowledged to the crowd that it was okay. It was okay. That simple shrug confirmed her understanding of how any proud father might become overwhelmed with emotion when he watched his son win a gold medal. Especially a son who entered the world with the odds stacked higher than anything Joey ever experienced in the ring.

Especially here, at the second-ever Special Olympics.

Carman, the entertainer, the chef and the clown.

Striking a famous Elvis pose, Carman belts out, "I'm All Shook Up" during a poolside party.

For a time Carman worked in a restaurant, but never the head chef as pictured here.

For charity events to raise money for local children's organizations, Carman transformed into "Carman-the-Clown," once a year. He's seen here with volunteer coworkers from Cherry Hill Township.

16

Carman Lights Up the World

Rosalie turned off the lights: Into the kitchen, she brought the cake, lit by eight flickering flames. When she placed the cake on the table, Carman quickly blew out the candles, and the gathering of family and friends applauded and burst into "Happy Birthday." Some of the party-goers vocalized softly, so they could hear an old neighbor's singing in particular. The reason was clear: They strained to hear fellow party-guest Frances Thomas Avallone, also known as former teen idol Frankie Avalon. The now 30-year-old Avalon actually lived in Hollywood, but his mother and father still resided in Cherry Hill, to which the Avallone and Tilelli families had moved from the same South Philadelphia street many years earlier.

Frankie Avalon, starring at Cherry Hill's famous Latin Casino nightclub, was only a five-minute ride from the Tilelli household. He was all too happy to headline Carman's surprise birthday party. Even at this young age, it was evident that Carman's localized fame would rise.

Carman's penchant for wit and entertainment was in full flight, and his ability to bring life to any function began early. Once, on a cruise, Joey and Rosalie turned around to see what Carman was doing. They found him onstage, entertaining the ship's passengers with his remarkable impersonations of Jimmy Durante—with whom Carman once had actually rubbed noses, backstage at the Spectrum, Carman getting the short end of that exchange—Ed Sullivan, and his all-time favorite, Elvis Presley.

The antics continued at school, where Carman apprenticed for a time in the printing shop. One day, he got a bright idea to produce notepads for a neighbor. When he presented the surprise gift to his friend, the man expressed appreciation. However, as soon as Carman left the home, the neighbor threw the stationery in the trash. The man didn't mean to slight Carman or demean the hard work. He simply didn't want his name and address on any of his notes or correspondence.

The man was a bookie.

One warm summer day, Carman's brothers Paul and Steve decided to build a fort in their backyard. Naturally, they needed lumber. They learned that a family down the street was adding a room onto their home. The brothers, including Carman, gathered a few freshly-cut two-by-fours, and lugged them behind their home. During the final trip, the owner of the lumber came upon the young plank-lifters and chased after them. The Tilelli boys escaped and then hid. Later, Carman walked back onto the street, where the neighbor confronted him, and asked if he knew the house where the stolen lumber lay hidden.

"Yes," responded Carman. He pointed in the direction of his own home. For whatever reason, the man never did approach the Tilelli house or retrieve his lumber.

When Paul and Steve approached drinking age, it wasn't beyond them to share a beer now and then with Carman. They always prefaced their offer with this caution: "Now Carm, don't tell Mom and Dad." Naturally, as soon as Carman walked in the door, he'd seek out his parents so he could brag: "We just had a couple of beers."

Wham! Joey and Rosalie dropped quick, heavy hammers on his brothers.

As many times as the boys wandered outside of the Tilelli rules. Carman never failed to own up to misdeeds. He was incapable of hiding the truth or telling an outright lie—a personality trait consistent with Down syndrome that perhaps kept his brothers from ever straying beyond the act of procuring a few planks that belonged to a neighbor.

The Mummers Tilelli—
Joey, Joseph, and Carman

Unless one was raised in Philadelphia or visited the city during New Year's Day, chances are the Mummers Parade means nothing. For natives of Philly, it has been a major tradition for centuries. Some date its origin to an ancient Roman festival. More likely, it dates back to mid-17th century English, Irish, German, or Swedish traditions.

The parade originally took place in Swedesboro, New Jersey, located near the Delaware Bay across from Philadelphia. In early America, Swedish settlers began parading the day after Christmas. Even the fledgling nation's President, George Washington, is said to have participated in the parade during his years while living in the nation's first capital—Philadelphia. In 1901, the city posted prize money, and created the first "official" Philadelphia parade of the modern era.

Today, the Mummers Parade consists of four divisions: Comics, Fancies, String Bands, and Fancy Brigades. The comics dress as clowns in colorful outfits (not dissimilar to Mardi Gras or the Italian *Carnevale*), carry umbrellas and generally parody a current theme, while Fancies march in elaborate costumes accompanied by a live band. String Bands play unamplified string and other instruments. The Fancy Brigades are larger groups of fancies but include grand, elaborate costumes and floats. They also follow a distinctive theme.

The parade has not endured without its controversies and detractors over the years. The firing of guns—"shooters"—was disallowed, as was the painting of blackface, although the marchers still perform the "Mummers' Strut" to a deep-rooted, southern plantation song, "Oh! Dem Golden Slippers." Also, women were not welcome in the ranks until 1970.

The "Mummers' Strut" resembles a cross between a baby's first steps and a drunk walking on a trampoline. In order to become a Mummer, it requires an adult to learn either how to walk like a baby again, or utilize the easier method; simply downing a few shots of liquor or many tankards of beer. The strut begins by grabbing onto one's outer garment, a coat or jacket, by the right lapel. It is held open wide so as to expose the Mummer's body to the frosty January air. Next, the body bends at the waist, leans to the right, and takes two or three sideward steps. This is best done in a tripping fashion. One then comes to a complete stop, grabs the left lapel and staggers back in the opposite direction. These steps should end one back where they began but for many it does not. A 360-degree turn is optional. If a coat isn't worn, an umbrella works just as well as opening a garment. It may even provide some necessary balance. (1)

Rosalie Tilelli grew up in South Philly, where the parade was organized every New Year's morning. "I loved the parade. The Mummers assembled early in the morning right outside my house. I was just a kid and I wanted to see the parade. But, Joey, he ruined it for me."

Joey interjected, "Yeah, just because I walked in the parade … she didn't like me in the parade."

"One year, we were living in Brooklyn and we stayed with my aunt in South Philly," Rosalie continued, "We went to a party New Year's Eve and Joey disappears. We're all wondering what happened to him. Then the next afternoon we saw this Mummer coming down the street toward my aunt's house."

The Mummer's outfit appeared to be simply a pair of men's black pajamas. An oriental coolie hat tilted precariously on his head. He had mastered the Mummers' Strut expertly and assuredly by following the imbibing method over baby-steps. The Mummer seemed lost, as he was far from the parade route and the rest of the revelers. It became obvious that this marcher had simply become exhausted, and now wandered in the general direction of a bed. Quite pleased with himself, his smile grew wider as his eyelids slid downward. Fortunately, the eyes remained open long enough to find his aunt's home. Rocking back and forth, side to side, like a juggler on a unicycle, he climbed the three front steps of the South Philly row house and opened the door. Joey greeted his wife and family, exclaiming:

"I'm Tokyo Joe!"

He flopped on the sofa and quickly fell asleep. Rosalie remembered, "After that, I hated the Mummer's Parade. Hated it!"

Rosalie had a change of heart in the mid-1970s when Joseph, her eldest son, became a Mummer. Her thawing sentiments became complete when Joseph asked Carman if he'd like to join his club and march in the annual event. Carman loved the Mummers and could not contain his enthusiasm. According to Joseph, when told of the offer to join, Carman's joyful expression soared far beyond anything Joseph could ever remember seeing during an entire lifetime of the two growing up together.

A club member does not just show up on New Year's Day. For some, Mummery is a way of life. Right after the parade, the groups perform in major shows. Throughout the year, smaller groups play at weddings, birthdays, confirmations, bar mitzvahs, and even funerals. They hold weekly or monthly meetings to plan the next year's costumes and theme. Members frequently socialize together. More than one divorce is attributable to membership in a Mummers' club, where imbibing one's favorite alcoholic beverage is the predominant activity—especially while marching on Philly's bitter cold New Year's mornings.

For an entire year, Carman attended regular meetings with Joseph. He became more and more animated as the big day approached. He couldn't stand still the day he was fitted for his costume—a clown.

Carman climbed out of bed at 4:00 a.m. on New Year's Day, 1975. Joseph arrived a half-hour later to drive him from Cherry Hill to South Philadelphia and their club's staging area. Carman pulled on his clown suit, managed to sit still long enough for someone to apply his makeup, rolled through a final rehearsal, then headed to the starting point.

Joey and Rosalie sat in the stands along Broad Street and

anxiously awaited Carman's debut in the grandest pageant of all for a Philadelphian, the New Year's Day Mummers Parade, featuring "Carman the Clown."

Throughout the years, marchers performed who could strut better, but none enjoyed it more. Joey jumped out of his seat when he saw Carman—his excitement nearly as overwhelming as Carman's. Rosalie also enjoyed the parade. She watched with tremendous pride as her son, whom doctors once predicted would cause conflict in the home, ignited an entire parade route with his most enthusiastic rendering of the Mummers' Strut.

Joey laughed and cheered. This time, he didn't cry for Carman's success. Good thing: The tears would have frozen on his face.

(1) The degree of public drunkenness during the parade has been severely curtailed over the past few decades. As the prize money increased, sobriety has been stressed, maintained, and enforced by the various organizations.

The "Night of Champions." Giardello, center wearing suit, and Carman, next to his dad, are surrounded by boxing champions before charity bouts held at Philadelphia's Spectrum, March, 1972. The bouts raised funds for special needs children including Joey's favorite charities, St. John of God School and the Special Olympics.

17

A Gathering of Old Friends

In early 1972, Joey placed calls to his old friends. He wanted to stage an even bigger "Night of Champions" for charity than the one he'd held in 1969. Instead of inviting eight "old time" boxers, he phoned twenty. All of them answered the call. This time, the famous fighters' names would blaze on the marquee above South Philadelphia's Spectrum.

Spectrum fans have witnessed terrific fights over the years, thanks to promoters who presented some magnificent cards. They matched their money-making concern with a deep pride in honoring and continuing Philadelphia's rich boxing tradition. To wit, the first fight in the Spectrum ring featured Philly's own "Smokin' Joe" Frazier. Frazier's three fights with Muhammad Ali remain perhaps the most universally known component of heavyweight championship fighting lore. Other greats who battled in the Spectrum have included Roberto Duran, Willie "The Worm" Monroe, Mike Tyson, Bernard Hopkins, Mathew Saad Muhammad, Marvin Hagler, and Bennie Briscoe.

For the film, *Rocky*, the Los Angeles Memorial Sports Arena was transformed into the Spectrum where Rocky, played by native-born Philadelphian Sylvester Stallone, first took on opponent Apollo Creed, played by Carl Weathers.

Even against that impressive backdrop, no Philly promoter or film director will ever surpass the dream slate assembled for charity by Joey Giardello. From boxing's Golden Age, he gathered Carmen Basilio, Jake LaMotta, Rocky Graziano, Willie Pep, Sandy Saddler, Chico Vejar, Charley Fusari, Billy Graham, Ernie Durando, Billy Conn, Frank Franconeri, Freddie Russo, Tippy Larkin, Chuck Davey, Eddie Giosa, Larry Forte, Paul Pender, Bat Battalino, and "Jersey" Joe Walcott. The card shimmered with championship-belt gold and Halls of Fame credentials; between them, these boxers once held eight world titles. Promoter Al Certo and many others participated as judges, referees, and corner men. Fighters, promoters, and handlers donated their services for the love of Joey and his charities. They also buried once-torrid animosities, as some of these fighters had grave issues with one another inside and outside the ring. Joey was far from immune, as some developed serious grudges during their fighting days that could have remained long after they retired.

For the second time in four years, all grudges evaporated for the "Night of Champions" and its beneficiaries—retarded children's organizations.

Joey delights in telling a story about a fellow boxer whom he met during his early days in the ring. "We were training at the same camp up in the Poconos. We got quite friendly and played cards after the workouts. Well, when it came to the fight, I beat him. I bump into him again after, and he seems kind of mad. So I say to him, 'Look, it was only a fight.' He stares back and says. 'Joey, I ain't mad about the fight. I'm still burning because you beat me at gin rummy.'"

Willie Pep and Sandy Saddler now fought for a sixth time, twice for Joey's charities and four for real. In their last real fight where they were both suspended for "wrestling," September 26, 1951, the referee even got knocked down at one point during the bizarre bout.

Most boxers left their anger inside the ring. After fights, they could be the best of friends. Not everyone was consumed by bitterness.

The charity bouts were hardly representative of the incredible brawls these guys had staged in their prime. Most combatants arrived at the venue overweight, out of shape, and winded by climbing into the ring. They wore oversized 16-ounce gloves and jabbed harmlessly at each other. Some guys added a little comedy by launching wild punches at the referee or chasing him out of the ring. During his bout, Freddie Russo landed two solid downward angled rights to the knee of Frank Franconeri as the bell sounded to end the second round. The punches had the desired effect of lowering Frank's shorts as he returned to his corner. Embarrassed, Frankie raced out for the beginning of the third round, grabbed Freddie Russo's toupee, and threw it over the ropes into the crowd. That prank produced the biggest laugh of the night.

Some 4,000 fans paid their way into the arena—a far better turnout than the 1,500 who watched the first "Night of Champions." All of the profits were donated to local associations for retarded children. Once again, the fighters paid their own expenses, and none received an appearance fee. Jake "The Bronx Bull" LaMotta expressed his feelings after the event. "Fighters are good guys. We do a lot for kids. That's just what we do."

Before he left the arena, Chico Vejar invited the boxers to join him on his upcoming Christmas Eve trip to spread cheer to children in a poor Appalachian mining town. Five immediately agreed: Joey, Willie Pep, Charlie Fusari, Ernie Durando, and Tippy Larkin. Chico later obtained commitments from Joey Archer, Steve Belloise, and Ralph "Tiger" Jones. The nine retired boxers all knew that the decision to travel out of town on Christmas Eve would not be popular at home. But as Jake LaMotta stated, *"This is just what we [ex-fighters] do."*

Rosalie left her ringside seat and headed for the exit right after the bouts, while Carman followed his father to the locker room for the group photo shoot. Carman nestled between Joey and the renowned Willie Pep. Surrounded by so many greats from the Golden Era of Boxing, the photographer needn't have said, "Say cheese," as Carman's 18-year-old lips could not have spread any farther. Furthermore, he was the primary reason why these battle-

141

weary fighters had laced up the gloves one more time. They boxed for Carman Tilelli and for one of their own, his dad, Joey Giardello.

The phone rang early on Christmas Eve morning in 1972, very early. Too early. Willie Pep knew who was on the line before he answered.

"Yes, Chico."

Chico Vejar wanted to know if Willie had remembered his promise to visit Appalachia. He did, but harbored second thoughts about leaving. The fact that it was Christmas Eve didn't matter so much to Willie. He wanted to stay home because he had just moved into a new house in Wethersfield, Connecticut. Stacks of unpacked boxes sat before him. "But, I like to do these things, and for Chico, I couldn't say no," remembered Willie.

After a quick breakfast, Willie left the house and drove to Jack Dempsey's restaurant in Manhattan to pick up Steve Belloise. Steve was always willing to help out, as he had for Joey's Philadelphia benefit nine months earlier. Together they headed for Al Certo's Custom Tailor Shop in Secaucus, New Jersey. There, Willie and Steve hooked up with Ernie Durando, Tippy Larkin, Charley Fusari, and Ralph "Tiger" Jones.

Planning for this trip began months earlier when Chico Vejar learned about the plight of some children in a welfare hospital in the heart of the poverty-stricken Appalachia region. The hospital was poor, almost as poor as the families that had children there. Chico decided that they would have a Christmas they would always remember ... He begged for toys and clothing from department stores. He begged for candy from candy manufacturers. And he got it all, including the use of an executive private jet. Everybody had opened their hearts and their pocketbooks for the kids and their families.

Chico also got a list of what was needed: wheelchairs and braces, etc. He also learned what clothes sizes were needed for individual families and also the ages of the kids for toys. He even sent twin beds to one family. (The family) had a handicapped daughter and what little money was left over from their food bills had to go for her; so their two sons had to sleep on mattresses on the floor. And it's cold down there.

Chico got everything together and most of the stuff was shipped on down ahead. (1)

Al Certo paid his highly-skilled tailors who designed, cut, and sewed suits for many celebrities, including champions like Jack Dempsey, to take time from their paying work to create well-fitting Santa elves and clown suits for the boxers heading to Appalachia to spread Christmas cheer. Each boxer dressed in his costume. Chico donned Santa's outfit. Ernie Durando, Tippy Larkin, and Charley Fusari dressed as clowns, and Willie Pep, Steve Belloise, and "Tiger" Jones as elves.

After dressing, they headed for the Newark New Jersey Airport, where the two Joeys, Giardello and Archer, awaited them. The plane took off for Pottsville, Pennsylvania, loaded with boxes of toys, along with wheelchairs, leg braces, and clothing already sized for the children they'd visit.

When the plane landed in Pottsville, representatives from the Cerebral Palsy, Heart, Polio, and Leukemia foundations met the plane with full itineraries in hand. The boxers split into groups, some visiting hospitals and others traveling to individual homes. Santa Chico carried a big bag of toys slung over his shoulder; "elves" Steve Belloise and Joey Archer walked through the wards distributing presents. They dispensed robes, slippers, pajamas, and lots of toys to the wildly excited kids. Most of the gifts were donated, but the boxers also bought many of the presents themselves.

Joey visited a private home and watched two sisters, ages 12 and 14, try on their new coats to replace the tattered, torn jackets they had been wearing. They told Joey that they couldn't wait to go back to school after the holidays so they could show off their coats. Joey had to fight back tears, as did some of the other boxers during their visits.

The crippled, sick, and impoverished children who were visited by these men from the brutal boxing business would never forget this particular Christmas.

On the flight back to Newark, the men were quiet in their individual thoughts. Joey recalled Jake LaMotta's words. "This is just what we do."

After the plane landed, Willie Pep remained in his elf costume. He rolled down his window as he drove off from the airport and yelled, "Merry Christmas, ya lousy bums."

Joey arrived home at 8:30 p.m., thankful that it was still Christmas Eve and he'd made it home for Rosalie, Carman, and the other boys, Joseph, Paul, and Steve. He'd honored his commitment to a grateful Chico Vejar and a more grateful number of happy children in Appalachia. He and the other *lousy bums* cared enough to take the time, donate the money, and visit a few of those less fortunate. This is what they do—these tough guys.

(1) *Friday's Heroes.* Willie Pep, *ibid.*

Cherry Hill, New Jersey Township's Mayor Platt escorts "the man" into the renamed community center during Carman's 2005 retirement ceremony.

18

The Workaholic Enters Valhalla

Carman walked out of his home determined to find employment. He had been granted a diploma from Cherry Hill West High School, even though he'd received his education and training at St. John of God School in nearby Westville Grove. The official parchment was the result of a New Jersey state law that provided proof of education from the community's school system, even though Carman had earned it from a nontraditional educational facility. While Carman hated to leave St. John of God at age 21, there was little more the school could offer him, plus legally he was required to leave. It was time for Carman to move on and get a job.

In his customary manner when embarking on a personal quest, he asked for no help from family, friends, or teachers. He received none. His unorthodox job search consisted of walking around town and looking for an opportunity. The first circumstances that confronted him did not arise from a job prospect but a chance to demonstrate how strong he'd grown. He entered a weight-lifting contest. Never one to skip a challenge, Carman stepped up and power-lifted his way to a trophy. He returned home, placed the trophy on the mantle next to Joey's bronzed, championship gloves, and left the house again to continue his job search, hoping that no additional obstacles would get in his way.

Carman burst forth with so much confidence that it never occurred to him that he might encounter a job that he could not handle. He possessed this confidence because Joey, Rosalie, and his teachers at St. John of God School emphasized that he should go out and just reach for the stars.

✳ ✳ ✳

The Cherry Hill Municipal building loomed over Carman. The two-story, red-brick structure was impressive for a small suburban town. This was the seat of power in Cherry Hill, where the mayor worked, the city council met, and the police and courts conducted business. Anyone might feel a little apprehensive about walking into the building without a scheduled appointment—but not "the man," Carman, who followed his quest with passion. He desired a job, so he marched up the steps and right into City Hall.

Once inside, Carman didn't see a reception area. Had he continued to walk straight, he would have marched out the back door. To the left and right, he surveyed long hallways filled with people scurrying in both directions. He chose to climb the stairway and found himself on the second-floor-landing with more perplexing choices—Traffic Court, Tax Office, Judge Levin, City Council, and Office of the Mayor. Carman turned right and walked directly toward Mayor John Rocco's office.

At the office of the mayor, Carman was steered to the right people, filled out an application, and was hired. He started work on June 28, 1978. He was assigned to the custodial department. Officially, Carman was a part-time employee. He worked from 8:30 a.m. to 4:30 p.m. each and every weekday even though, he knew, he could have left before the lunch hour. He never took advantage, always working beyond his rightful quitting time.

One winter day, it began to snow around noon; by late afternoon, Carman and others looked out to see nearly white-out conditions. Mayor Rocco decided to close down the building early and assign crews to clean off the steps and sidewalks before releasing the workers. Inside the community center, Carman's job required that he break down tables and chairs that had been utilized during the day. Needing help for the task, he stuck his head outside and asked one of the sidewalk cleaners to assist. Out of respect for Carman, and perhaps the chance for a warmer, softer job, the employee gladly joined Carman inside. Next day, the employee was read the riot act by his supervisor because the sidewalk-clearing task should have taken precedence over Carman's request.

When the supervisor approached Carman about the incident, he got flustered. He nearly broke into tears. Since Carman had known that everyone would be going home early the previous day, he felt that he needed to complete his assigned task in order to finish before dismissal. The supervisor never could have convinced Carman that the tables and chairs might well have been broken down and stored the next day, so he didn't try.

On another winter evening, Carman looked out from his bedroom window when snow began falling lightly. Flakes sparkled like fireflies as they crossed under a streetlight's illumination. A frosty coating covered the lawn but the streets appeared only wet. Car traffic passed by his house at normal speeds, windshield wipers set to intermittent. Carman giggled softly. He slid down into his bed, smiled, and pulled up the covers; he loved snow. He could already see himself after work, clearing the snow off the family's back-yard pool and ice skating before dinner. The spectacle of so much fun made it tough for Carman to fall asleep, but sleep came.

Waking at 5:30 a.m., Carman sprang up and peered out the window. It seemed as if the Arctic tundra had migrated six thousand miles south and descended upon Cherry Hill. The lawn, driveway, sidewalk, and street were a continuous white-covered expanse. Judging by the now near-invisible bicycle Carman's brother had leaned against a tree, the snow piled nearly four feet high. Carman quietly inched out of bed, dressed in his uniform, pulled on his boots, heavy galoshes, and parka, and slipped out the back door. He didn't want to wake anyone, especially his mom, whom he knew would try to keep him home. Carman trudged the half mile to City Hall and waited for someone to come who could open the doors. No one came. Some snow days were bad enough that even city hall shut down. Disappointed, Carman slogged home after an hour-long wait.

✳ ✳ ✳

Carman's immediate superior for the last 15 years of his employment at City Hall, Gary Kanefsky, enjoyed the company of his extroverted, notorious worker. He loved to tell outlandish stories about Carman:

"All during the week throughout the day, three different groups utilized the community center: The Mature Club, Super Senior Club, and the Retired Men's Club. They all loved Carman to death. One or two curmudgeons might complain about something once in a while, but they were the type who would complain about anybody.

"When Carman would set up the community center for a function and audio equipment was required. I would do a 'one, two, one, two' for a sound check, then I'd ask Carman to do one. Rather than one, two, one, two, he'd do his famous Elvis imitation. With a curled lip, and a full, Elvis-hip gyration he'd sing. 'I'm All Shook Up.' He might not always get the lyrics right but for that moment, he *was* Elvis. Over all the years that he held the job, Carman never failed to do Elvis when I asked for a sound check.

"On his birthday we'd have a small party, and he'd collect about $250 from club members. Then he'd say that it was his birthday every day all week— looking for more money. He cracked us up.

"His specific job was custodial; he'd clean the floors, the bathrooms, and kitchen of the community center. He'd remove the trash, set up and tear down the tables and chairs for functions. For all intents and purposes he ran the custodial department of Cherry Hill Township.

150

"I couldn't have picked anyone more reliable. Any days that he missed were the direct result of his parents keeping him home for whatever reason. I don't recall him ever missing a day on his own. He'd come in sick. When his parents sent notice that they were taking him on vacation, he'd come to me and say in his sweet way, 'I don't really want to go.'

"Once a year, due to a union contract, the custodial and maintenance personnel were allowed a new pair of boots. While Carman was not officially entitled to new boots, I made sure that Carman was included. Now Carman had very small feet, so we would try his boots on and ask him to walk around; when he said 'fine' we'd leave [the shoe store]. Then the next day, each year, without fail, his mom would stick a note in a boot and send them back in the box, telling me that they hurt his feet.

"So the following year I took him to get his boots. I told him to walk in them. I took him to the community center and told him to do his job in them. They were finally okay. The next day he came in and complained that they hurt. I looked down and they were on the wrong foot. After a quick change, the world became right once again for Carman.

"Whenever his family went on vacation Carman would inform me of the dates, usually a week in duration. One year Joey and Rosalie informed Carman that he'd be away from work for ten days. Carman bitterly complained. 'Ten days!'

"He told me that he really didn't want to go; that he'd rather come to work. Carman truly loved his job and the people who worked at City Hall. In return, the mayors, councilmen, councilwomen, judges, and coworkers all loved him back.

"Carman was a great kidder. Most employees were not quick enough to come back against the dynamite one-liners he'd throw at them. And rank had no privilege. He'd shout at me. 'Here he comes, the boss, half-man and half-woman.' This incident happened at a time when I had allowed my hair to flow below my shoulders.

"I think you can be loved in more than one way. Carman was loved at home differently than he was here. His father may have been a disciplinarian with unconditional love, but here he had people who just embraced him for the joy of embracing him unconditionally. Here he got a different kind of love, one he earned.

"Here's a guy who [was] technically disabled but someone whom we could learn from. I learned from Carman Tilelli. His work ethic was better than anybody else in this building. He was the complete conscience employee. He knew when it was necessary to come get me. He just knew without being told when a problem required my attention. Carman was as independent as you could imagine for a man with Down syndrome.

"The things that you could learn from Carman were far and above anything that you might learn from anyone else here.

"There was no one in the building that didn't know Carman. There are about 70 people here in City Hall, not counting some 120 police officers.

"One of my regrets is that after Carman retired, I had hoped to bring him back on occasion to the men's clubs, but he wasn't physically able to do that very shortly after he retired," Kanefsky concluded.

As he relayed the stories, Kanefsky's face displayed the hurt and disappointment his management decision to retire Carman still caused him, many years after making it. This group of township employees, especially his boss, didn't merely mouth the words. Their love for Carman radiated throughout the buildings.

Lou DiCiurcio, a Cherry Hill Township retired police detective and family friend knew first-hand that Carman was a major league prankster. "I'd be at lunch and Carman would come into my area, empty the trash can, then he'd place the receptacle on my chair. For good measure, he'd take my glasses off the desk and hide them under my in-box. Sometimes I'd see him coming and I'd hide and catch him in the act. He'd give me that look—'What? What did I do?' He was a real practical joker."

Detective Sergeant Joseph Vitarelli, Jr. added, "But everybody loved Carman, everybody! He had special sayings. For instance, once I took him to my brother's restaurant. Ever since that day, every day thereafter when he'd come up, Carman would yell, 'How about free pizza?' He'd call me Joe Vic. 'Joe Vic, how about some free pizza?'"

Another officer, Kyle Brooks, chimed in. "I'll tell you though, Carman was very sharp. He knew what was going on. You couldn't put anything over on him."

Lou went on to tell how Carman loved the girls. "On, his birthday, he'd come up here with a big smile and lipstick covering his entire face. To one gal named Honey, he'd say, 'Honey, she's my wife!'"

The police officers all laughed, but when talk turned to Carman's retirement, one heard their voices soften and felt the anguish as they lamented that, after 27 years, Carman could no longer perform his duties: But that wasn't the principal issue—the officers all feared that Carman might get hurt. And they all loved him too much to give the issue a pass. His equilibrium began to go and his memory slipped. A maintenance coworker reported that Carman had been asked to sweep the steps in front of the municipal building and minutes later ended up blocks away by a baseball field and had to be brought back.

On another occasion, Carman acknowledged to a concerned coworker that he had become dizzy and that he may have even temporarily passed out. Knowing that a blackout might lead to problems for him, Carman begged the coworker not to tell his mother. But that was a request his coworker, no matter how much it hurt, could not honor.

Carman may have been all too keenly aware that his days working for the municipality were nearing an end.

The time for Carman's retirement finally had arrived with certainty. But the legendary Carman, "the man," lives on in the halls of the police department, the courts, the community center, and all the offices. From the mayor to the maintenance workers, Carman's legendary personality and wild exploits remain topics for nostalgic discussions to this day, wherever one roams throughout Cherry Hill's Municipal Buildings.

❊ ❊ ❊

In early 2005, it became painfully certain to Kanefsky that Carman could no longer safely perform his duties. He informed Rosalie that the day would soon be forthcoming when he would have to ask Carman to retire. By midyear, Kanefsky decided that by year's end, Carman would be asked to retire. It was an excruciating task, but a necessary one. Kanefsky planned to hold a retirement party for Carman in December. He proposed an idea to Mayor Bernie Platt: to rename the community center building where Carman had labored for 27 years the "Carman Tilelli Community Center." Mayor Platt had known Carman over the course of three decades, as he was the second and final mayor during Carman's tenure with Cherry Hill Township.

"I called him 'Carmy' and he called me 'Bernie,'" said Mayor Platt. "Gary (Kanefsky) told me 'Carmy' was slipping and that he had no choice but to ask him to retire. Gary brought me the idea to name the community center after Carman at his retirement party. I embraced the idea, and it was a formality to ask council to go along. In addition, we declared his retirement ceremony 'Carman Tilelli Day' in Cherry Hill Township.

"I watched his progress for some thirty years, and there was not one person in this building that didn't love him. He never lost a day's work. He was prompt. He was as good an employee as ever worked here. He was a wonderful human being. We knew his life would change, because every day before his retirement he had something to look forward to. I'm so glad that we were a part of Carman's life and glad that we made his days worthwhile."

Gary Kanefsky planned perhaps the one of the best days ever for Carman, but also one that would surely hurt his most devoted and beloved employee. With the blessing of Mayor Platt and the City Council, Kanefsky planned for Carman's retirement party. The date was set for December 21, 2005. Kanefsky personally purchased the letters and carefully placed them over the community center's double doors. He covered the name over with a white cloth. "I was very careful to spell his name correctly," he said. For good reason; many over the years had spelled Carman, "Carmen," or like his father, Joey's legal first name, "Carmine."

On the big day of Carman's retirement party, he arrived at work with Joey and Rosalie. They were seated in the center of the front row inside the community center. The mayor gave a short talk, lauding Carman for his 27 years of service and declared it "Carman Tilelli Day" in Cherry Hill Township. The room erupted in applause and Carman was given a standing ovation. Joey buried his head; tears swelled in his eyes as they usually did whenever Carman was honored. The assembly then walked outside, formed a ring around Carman, and looked up. Carman was handed a lanyard which he pulled. The cloth dropped and revealed the building's new name:

C-A-R-M-A-N   T-I-L-E-L-L-I

C-O-M-M-U-N-I-T-Y   C-E-N-T-E-R

Shock, bewilderment, and glee showed in rapid succession across Carman's cherubic, 52-year-old face.

Gary Kanefsky summed up the moment. "To watch Joey Giardello, with his head down in tears, as we gave Carman a standing ovation … it was a sight to behold."

Years later, still emotional about dismissing Carman, Kanefsky said, "I hope Joey and Rosalie know that we did our best to care for him. His safety was much more of a concern than the tasks he performed near the end of his career. We'd all cover for him and helped do his job for him, if required, but he began to lose his equilibrium and we had to ask him—actually I notified his parents— to retire. It was a very sad day. We were very much aware of how much this job meant to him and how it would adversely affect his psyche, but I didn't have a choice. His legs were going and his mind was slipping, too. It was strictly a safety issue. What do you do? I think that I made the correct decision."

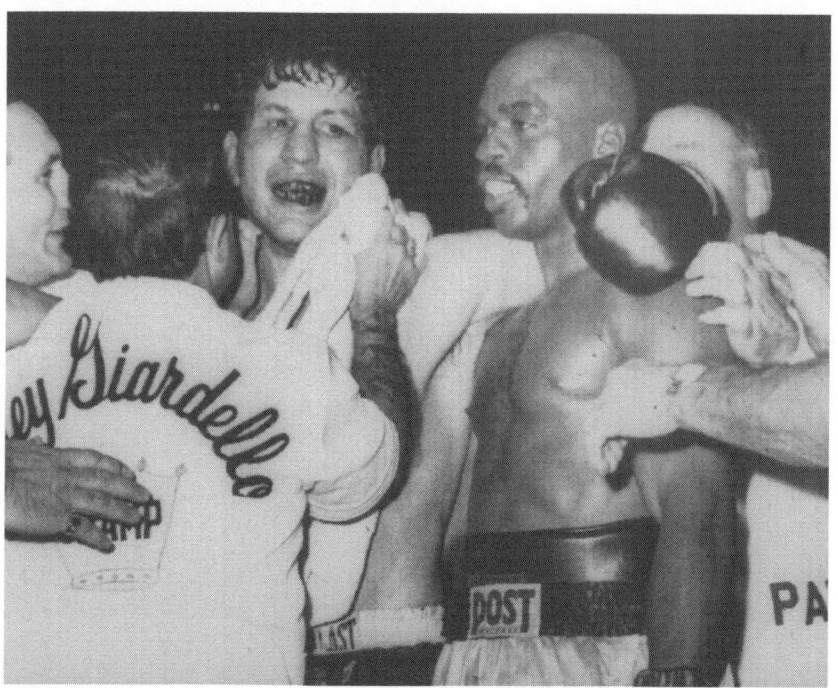

Giardello hugs Rubin "Hurricane" Carter after successful defense of middleweight title, December 1964. This fight is featured, Hollywood-style, in a 1999 movie starring Denzel Washington as Carter. The film caused a great deal of controversy when it depicted Carter winning, and then denied the crown citing racism.

19

Withstanding the Hurricane

Joey girded himself for the grueling task ahead. It was January 2000, five years before the ceremony for his son that would bring him one of the happiest moments of his life. Joey just hated to sue people. He recalled the suit against the New York Athletic Boxing Commission over the Billy Graham fight, which Joey won, thus shifting a loss over to the "win" column. He well remembered the depositions and trial for the gas station assault. Then there was the defense he presented against the $100,000 suit by the passenger who was hurt in the New Jersey Parkway accident. Collectively, these memories tightened Joey's stomach into knots. The last thing he wanted was another lawsuit and deposition, followed by an arduous trial. "I never liked to sue anybody; sue the fight game," said Joey.

But this time, it was absolutely necessary. His legacy was at stake, a legacy born of his challenging toil in the ring. His Hall of Fame reputation, built upon 20 years as a modern-day gladiator, had been permanently tarnished. He simply had to sue Universal Studios for the misrepresentation of the fight scene in the movie between himself and Rubin Carter—*The Hurricane*—starring Denzel Washington as Rubin "Hurricane" Carter.

Joey had obtained counsel from one of Philly's best, attorney

George Bochetto, no stranger to boxing, as he had served on the Pennsylvania Boxing Commission from 1995 to 2001. Many recognized Bochetto's accomplishments; *Philadelphia Magazine* would name him as its "Super Lawyer" in 2004, 2005, 2007, and 2008.

For Joey, this issue was not a greedy grab for money. "I thought the movie belittled me. I fought so many fights [133] for so many years [19], with all my heart, and this movie makes a mockery of that," Joey told reporter Bernard Fernandez in a January 14, 2000, *Philadelphia Daily News* article. Attorney Bochetto agreed. "His primary concern was not the money. Joey had a lifestyle that was very established, his house was paid for, had the same wife for 50 years. He was very comfortable. It had absolutely nothing to do with money."

Nonetheless, the firm of Bochetto & Lenztz must have appeared to Joey as a sure winning lottery ticket. The firm's website boasted gargantuan medical practice settlements and personal injury, fraud, and defamation-of-character wins in the millions and multimillions such as the $10.7 million won for former world heavyweight contender Randall "Tex" Cobb against Time Inc., for a *Sports Illustrated* story. "What so upset Joey was that he believed that he's given his family a legacy—his kids, grandchildren, and those about him of being a world champion and having really accomplished something that very few people have ever accomplished," said Bochetto.

A few days after watching the movie, Bochetto told the *Philadelphia Daily News*, "Having been engaged by Mr. Giardello to represent him, I am looking at the factuality of the case very seriously. I am very concerned about the way in which Mr. Giardello has been treated [in the film]. I anticipate making an announcement very soon as to what we will do about it." In the same article, Suzanne Ellis, a spokeswoman for Beacon Communications, which produced the film, said the company had "no comment at this time on Giardello's threat of a lawsuit."

A week later, Bochetto, on behalf of Carmine O. Tilelli a/k/a, Joey Giardello, filed a civil action in the United States District Court for the Eastern District of Pennsylvania, against Universal Pictures, Beacon Communications, and Azoff Films.

The deposition took place in Philadelphia and Rosalie feared the toll that the legal wrangling would take on her husband. "They [Universal Studios] had their sharks come up from Washington. They had $5,000 suits on. They went into his childhood, why he had lied about his name going into the service. They had to videotape how he lied to get into the service. Joey can't take that kind of stuff. It wasn't good for him," explained Rosalie.

"I got the worst of it. They had to go thoroughly through my childhood," said Joey. "I had a good family. I had a father that was very strict. I was raised the right way."

The Universal Studios lawyer, Gerson A. Zweifach of Williams & Connolly, attempted to rattle Joey by showing the closing seconds of the Giardello/Carter fight film sequence over and over again. The exercise had the desired effect. "One time they showed that fight scene part of the film, and Joey wanted to go over the table and hit the lawyer," Rosalie recalled.

"Oh, it was terrible. They were trying to get Joey excited and wanted him to say something that would not play right in front of a jury," Bochetto said. "But it didn't work. We had Joey prepared for that."

Joey persevered through the depositions. He had no choice; his legacy was at stake. The lawsuit, depositions and pending trial created a great deal of publicity. Public attention is considered good and welcomed by motion picture studios, even when the reason for the heightened awareness might appear to be negative. In this case, Rosalie felt the opposite happened. "I think the publicity caused Denzel Washington to lose the Academy Award because there was so much controversy."

Attorney Bochetto demanded all versions of the screenplay—from the first draft to the last shooting script, including any minor or ad-libbed changes. In a typical Hollywood picture, this amounts to 15 to 25 versions, with writers other than the credited writer involved. It also included corrections made to staging and dialogue during the shooting. Bochetto felt if he could show how the script changed over the course of the production, that the progression might show how the director, the esteemed Norman Jewison (who also directed *In the Heat of the Night, Fiddler on the Roof, Jesus Christ Superstar, Agnes of God, Moonstruck,* and many other films), and the producers built up the fight scene to increase the appearance of a lopsided fight in favor of "Hurricane" Carter over Giardello. The attorney wanted to show where they might have piled on for dramatic effect, having the announcer declare Carter the winner before the decision was rendered. Which in the real fight never happened. Bochetto also wanted to reveal when they might have added the booing of the Philadelphia crowd, Giardello's *home* crowd, when he was announced the winner. "They got the crowd booing me. How could they do that? Nobody booed," Joey recalled. "Those were my people there from South Philly. They were happy I won. And I did win. I won, he lost. End of story."

The television announcer for the actual fight, Les Keiter, reported that the 15th round was nothing like the one shown in the movie. If anything, the real 15th round was the opposite of how it appeared in theatres. "The scene was absolutely, totally fictitious. I have my call of the fight on tape," he said. "And as for the fans booing Joey, don't be ridiculous. Nobody was going to do that to Giardello, in Philadelphia, especially after a fight he won and deserved to win."

Ron Lipton, once a 17-year-old Carter sparring partner and a close personal friend of Carter's, was called for a deposition. "I was supposed to do the choreography [for the fight scenes] and kept all my correspondence showing that I refused to make Giardello look like a bum and make it look like racial robbery. I lost the job because of my stand," stated Lipton in a Cyber Boxing Zone message board in 2005. He added, "The movie was total bullshit. I testified for eight hours straight. Joey G. sat right next to me."

In retrospect, Bochetto felt that subpoenaing the scripts may have tilted the case (along with Lipton's testimony) in Giardello's favor and caused Universal's attorney to back down. "They went through 20 variations of the screenplay. The evolution of the fight scene from reality to fiction [was] typified through all the different edits and changes and comments. And when I presented all that to them they knew that we'd made our case. They offered to settle."

On September 27, 2000, the *Philadelphia Daily News'* lead front and sports page story announced: "GIARDELLO SETTLES 'HURRICANE' SUIT." The article began, "Almost 33 years after his final professional bout, former middleweight champion Joey Giardello has the look of a winner again." (1)

The cash award of the settlement was not disclosed, but Joey, Rosalie, and George Bochetto expressed satisfaction. "Fortunately, we were able to get quite a bit of news coverage, so when the case settled and the defendants admitted being wrong and apologized to Joey, that got a lot of coverage. The apology made it onto the DVD version of the film, the interview with director Jewison. That, along with a fairly substantial payment of money, made Joey feel somewhat vindicated," explained Bochetto.

"For nineteen years, I fought the greatest fighters around, and I beat Carter fair and square. I just wanted to set the record straight and I think it has been," Joey added.

Rosalie was most relieved of all. "Thank Heavens—Joey would have never survived a trial," she confided.

Jewison expressed his views over the fight scene and the mandated requirement to add an apology to the DVD. "We just dealt with the last few seconds of the fight, where it seemed that Rubin had it. But going back over it, there's no doubt about it…Giardello won it."

Armyan Bernstein, co-founder of picture financier Beacon Communications, and co-author of the *The Hurricane* screenplay, wrote to Joey. "We had no intention of taking away from your legacy as world champion, or of besmirching the other boxing accomplishments in which you, your family and friends take pride." Perhaps in order to place part of the blame on Carter, the letter also stated, "Rubin Carter, who worked with us on 'The Hurricane,' told me that you never ducked a fight."

However, as Rosalie mentioned, the settlement and publicity may have caused the knockout of Denzel Washington from winning a1999 Academy Award and becoming the year's best actor. Kevin Spacey won that year for *American Beauty*. Denzel Washington had his day of redemption, however. In 2001, he won for *Training Day*. Ironically, he beat out Will Smith's riveting portrayal of world heavyweight champion Muhammad Ali in the biopic, *Ali*.

(1) Philadelphia Daily News, Bernard Fernandez. September 27, 2000

Joey got just as excited meeting other sports celebrities as others did when meeting him, here pointing to another great, Miami Dolphin's football Hall of Famer, Dan Marino. Marino is considered one of the greatest quarterbacks of all time.

20

Awards, Honors, and Retirement

After the excitement of *The Hurricane* movie, resultant lawsuit, and settlement, it proved time for the two champions, Carman and Joey, to retire and deservedly rest on their multiple laurels. Joey had achieved his life's goal of becoming middleweight champion of the world. His one regret: His father wasn't around to see and share the accomplishment. "I know he'd have been so proud," said Joey.

Joey retired from boxing, but boxing never tired of calling on him. He attended many championship fights and took his obligatory walk into the ring to wish the combatants well while fans remembered with respectful applause. He attended a few Sports Expos and autographed photos. Joey even attended a 1993 Hurricane Carter benefit in Las Vegas, where Carter was awarded an honorary World Boxing Council middleweight championship belt. Joey held no grudge against Carter for the fictitious movie scene, especially since Carter always stated, without reservation, that Joey had won the fight.

Joey left the ring, but he didn't retire from life; after all, he was not yet 40 years old. Like a few boxers before and after him, Joey received an offer to play a part in a movie. Called *Moonrunners*, the 1975 film starred James Mitchum, the son of and dead ringer for his famous father, Robert Mitchum. James appeared in 34 films but never achieved anywhere near the mega-star status of his father.

Joey's part was that of a "syndicate" man—the typical gangster-type as envisioned by a Hollywood casting director. However, they got it wrong. In Joey's big scene, his script read: "Tiny *ain't* gonna like this!" They were still filming after six takes as Joey corrected the grammar each time by offering, "Tiny *isn't* going to like this!" As we learned, Hollywood gets it wrong sometimes, perhaps more times than we'd like. The movie didn't set any box office record and its highlight may have been the original music score, written by Waylon Jennings. Joey acted in a commercial for a local rib joint, then let his Screen Actors Guild card lapse.

When Hollywood didn't call again, and it became apparent that Joey was not the next boxer/actor to follow in the footsteps of lesser boxing stars Jack Palance, Tony Danza, or Mickey Rourke, he commenced a search for a bona fide job. He took back his legal name, Carmine Tilelli, although most everyone still called him Joey, including Rosalie. Joey explored executive sales jobs marketing milk, chemicals, and insurance until he discovered his second career working for the state of New Jersey's division of weights and measures. Joey would spend 19 years with the State, traveling throughout southern New Jersey, handing out citations to supermarket owners who may have short-weighted vegetables, meats, and other store-packaged goods. The job fit Joey well, as he always enjoyed the role of enforcer for the little guy. He even cited a friend, Andy Lure, who owned two supermarkets in southern New Jersey. Andy explained that normal moisture evaporation can change a package's weight after a few days. Joey held his ground. "Andy, pay the fine and be more careful in the future," said Joey.

About this time, the phone began ringing on an almost annoying, regular daily basis. Rosalie usually answered.

RING! RING!

"Who is it, Hon?" Joey would ask.

Rosalie: "It's the Pennsylvania Sports Hall of Fame, they want to honor you."

RING! RING!

"Who is it, Hon?"

Rosalie: "It's the National Italian-American Sports Hall of Fame, they want to induct you."

RING! RING!

"Who is it, Hon?"

Rosalie: "It's the New Jersey Sports Hall of Fame. They want to fete you."

RING! RING!

"Who is it, Hon?"

Rosalie: "It's the Philadelphia Retired Boxers Association, another honor!"

Joey humbly and graciously accepted each award offered. He made every luncheon or dinner appearance and traveled to wherever the presentation required. Then in 1993, the big one came. The IBHO called.

RING! RING!

"Who is it, Hon?"

Rosalie: "The International Boxing Hall of Fame. Guess what they want?"

"What?

"They want to know if you can be in Canastota, New York, on June 13th?"

"What for? An appearance?"

"No, dear husband, for your induction!"

On Sunday, June 13, 1993, Joey Giardello was inducted into the International Boxing Hall of Fame, and received the gold Hall of Fame ring that symbolized his status as a Hall of Famer, alongside other immortals of boxing. His fellow modern inductees included Flash Elorde, Marvin Hagler, Harold Johnson, and Fritzie Zivic. Non-participants included, among others, Gil Clancy, Don Dunphy, and Teddy Brenner. It was Brenner who helped broker Joey's championship fight with Dick Tiger in Atlantic City, December 7, 1963.

"It was glorious weekend," recalled Rosalie, "hot but glorious." Joey didn't join the golf foursomes because he didn't believe that his golf game was good enough. "If I was younger, I would have conquered golf but I started playing late," said Joey. So he hung around the facility that day. "Yeah, they had him autograph stuff all day but it was a fun weekend," remembered Rosalie. Many of Joey's old pals were there from previous inductions, including good friends Willie Pep, Sandy Saddler, and Carmen Basilio—who, as a resident of Canastota, New York, was one of the major reasons why the International Boxing Hall of Fame was originally located there.

"Joey had his fists cast, which are kept at the Hall, and he received a beautiful, leather-bound certificate—and of course, a life-long prized possession—the ring," said Rosalie.

❊ ❊ ❊

Back home in Cherry Hill, the phone still kept ringing.
RING! RING!
"Who is it, Hon?"
"It's Cherry Hill Township, the mayor, Bernard Platt," answered Rosalie.
"Oh? What's he want?" asked Joey.
"He's requesting permission to rename a township building."
"After me?" questioned Joey.
"No, after our dear son, Carman!"
Cherry Hill Township renamed its recreation center the "Carman Tilelli Community Center" in December, 2005. Unlike when he received all those honors for himself, Joey cried at this dedication ceremony. Cried for his beloved over-achieving son who beat his disability to attain so much in life, including the remarkable accomplishment of having the "Tilelli" name honored in the family's own home town; a tribute that may endure longer even than those bestowed upon the father—Joey Giardello.

Epilogue

Carmine Tilelli, *a.k.a.* Joey Giardello, died of congestive heart failure, age 78, on September 4, 2008. Eulogies appeared in newspapers and magazines around the country and throughout the world. Rosalie received letters of condolences from friends and admirers of Joey, including Timothy Shriver, CEO of the Special Olympics and son of Special Olympics founder Eunice Shriver, and sports and boxing reporters across the globe.

Within days, the Veteran Boxers Association—Ring One (the oldest organization of its kind), along with the Harrowgate Boxing Club and Philly Boxing History, announced plans to erect a statue to perhaps the greatest middleweight to ever come out of Philadelphia.

Rosalie Tilelli was notified in the summer of 2009, during the writing of this book, that Joey would posthumously be inducted into Class VI of the Philadelphia Sports Hall of Fame. As in the case of his induction into the Philadelphia Chapter of the Italian-American Sports Hall of Fame, Giardello and Los Angeles Dodgers' player and coach, Norristown, Pennsylvania native Thomas Charles Lasorda, were entered together. "Joey would have been so proud of this honor," said Rosalie. "He loved all of the Philadelphia sports teams and the players. Lasorda loved to tease Carman; he'd say, 'Who's your favorite team—the Dodgers?' Carman would always come back, 'No, the Phillies!'"

On November 12, 2009, in addition to Giardello and Lasorda, sports notables Larry Bowa, Neil Johnston, Pete Retzlaff, John Cappelletti, and the entire 1974—1975 Philadelphia Flyers Hockey Stanley Cup Championship teams are among those inducted into Class VI. Giardello is only the third boxer to be inducted, the first two being Tommy Loughran, Class V (2008), and Joe Frazier, Charter Class (2004).

Joey Giardello was laid to rest on Wednesday, September 10, 2008 in his longtime hometown, Cherry Hill, New Jersey.

His brother, Bobby Tilelli, delivered these words at the funeral services:

> "At home he was not the renowned champion, just the man of the house. Rosalie made sure of that. He wasn't called 'Champ,' he was, 'Hon,' 'Pop' or 'Dad.' He never put on airs. What you saw in him was what you got. So we will leave it to the writers to extol Joey Giardello while we honor the man, Carmine Tilelli." In words borrowed from Shakespeare, Bobby concluded: *"His life was gentle, and the elements were so mixed within him that Nature might stand up and say to all the world. This was a man!"*

Realia

The Joey Giardello bronze statue sculpted by Carl LeVotch, located in South Philadelphia at the intersections of South 13th Street, Mifflin & East Passyunk, a few yards away where Giardello once trained.

Frankie Avalon, a neighbor from South Philadelphia, hugs his friend Carman.

Carman plants a kiss on "Uncle" Jake, one of the toughest men to ever enter the ring. Jake the "Bronx Bull" LaMotta, a former middleweight champion and a Hall of Famer, is best known today as the subject of the 1980 movie, Raging Bull, which starred Robert DeNiro as LaMotta.

Five-time-all-pro, New York Jets #99, Mark Gastineau, sees eye-to-eye with Carman. Mark tried his hand at boxing between 1991 and 1996, ending with a 15-2 record, although he never faced competition like Carman's dad.

Boy Scout Carman shakes hands with New Jersey governor, James Florio, once himself an amateur boxer. Florio held New Jersey's highest office from 1990-1994, and was a U. S. congressman for 15 years.

Joey and Rosalie sandwich New York Yankee legend Joe DiMaggio, who was once married to Marilyn Monroe. Joey and Joe remained good friends throughout their lives. DiMaggio's mother was also named Rosalie, and whenever the friends met, he never failed to ask about Carman.

*While in London for a fight in 1960, tourist Joey visited Trafalgar Square.
The bowler hat was needed where 35,000 pigeons once resided. A
later ban on feeding diminished and eventually eliminated the flock.*

Carman Tilelli worked a full shift every day for over 28 years when he could have quit right after lunch. When he retired in 2005, Cherry Hill Township named the community center in his honor.

Nobody was off limits for "Carman-the-Prankster" around Cherry Hill, New Jersey police HQ. He often placed detective Lou DiCiucio's trash can on his chair and would hide his reading glasses.

Carman points to the cast of his dad Joey Giardello's fist, on display for all to see at the Boxing Hall of Fame museum in Canastota, New York.

Giardello, not known as a knockout puncher, did manage to KO about 25% of his opponents. Here, an unidentified opponent is about to get a counting lesson from the referee as soon as he guides Joey to a neutral corner.

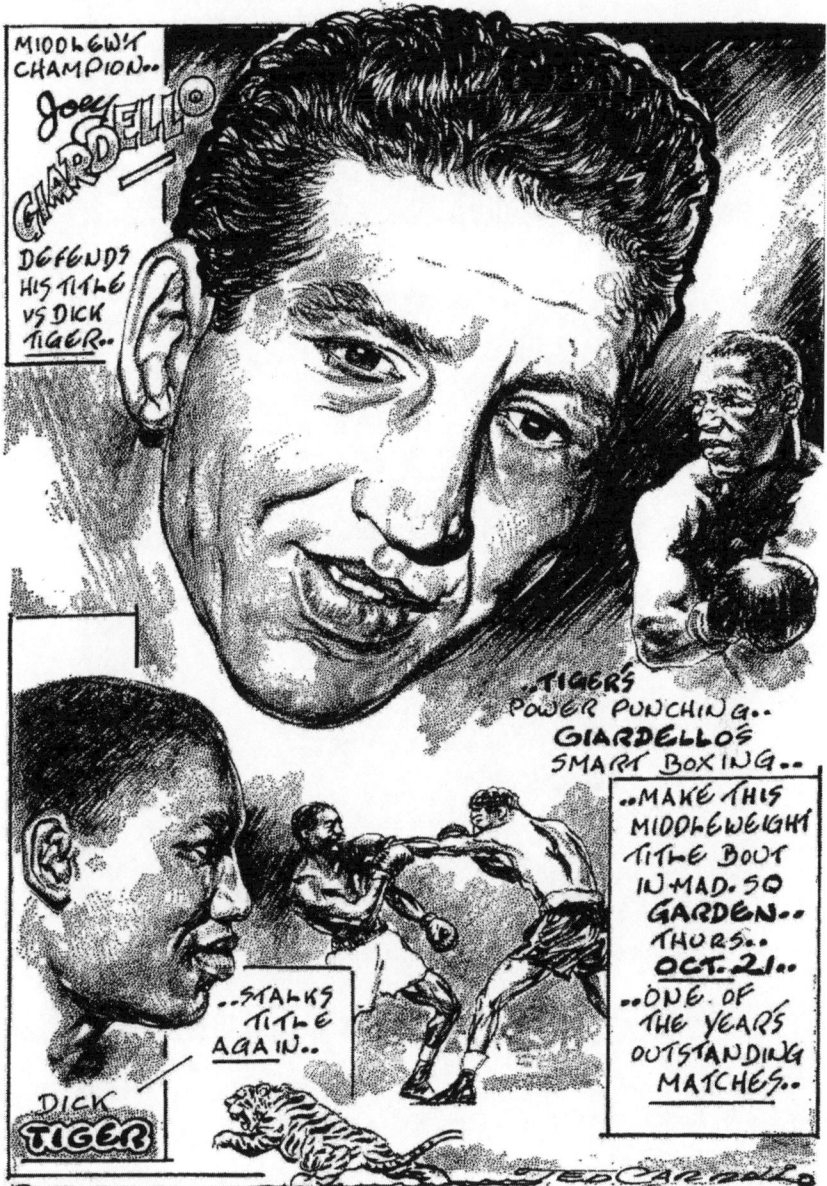

MADISON SQUARE GARDEN BOXING INC.
304 WEST 50TH ST.   NEW YORK, N. Y. 10019

Cartoonist depicts middleweight champ Giardello and challenger Dick Tiger. This, the fourth battle between them, went to Tiger, who reclaimed the title in October, 1965.

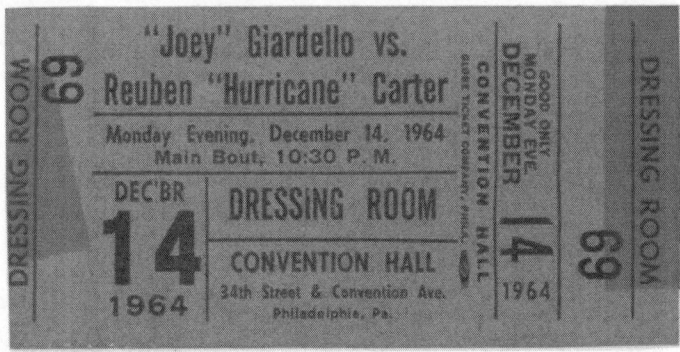

Worth far more than their face value, four tickets to Giardello's major fights, Giardello/Fullmer, April 20, 1960; Giardello/Robinson, June 24, 1963; Tiger/Giardello, December 7, 1963; Giardello/Carter, December 14, 1964. Note: Carter's first name was misspelled—"Reuben" instead of "Rubin."

The Tilelli men (l-r) Carman, Paul, Carmine (Joey), Steve, and Joseph.

"Tale of the Tape" for Tiger/Giardello championship fight, Atlantic City, December 7, 1963.

The Inaugural Committee

requests the honor of your presence

to attend and participate in the Inauguration of

John Fitzgerald Kennedy

as President of the United States of America

and

Lyndon Baines Johnson

as Vice President of the United States of America

on Friday the twentieth of January

one thousand nine hundred and sixty-one

in the City of Washington

Edward H. Foley
Chairman

Invitation to John Fitzgerald Kennedy's presidential inaugural ball.

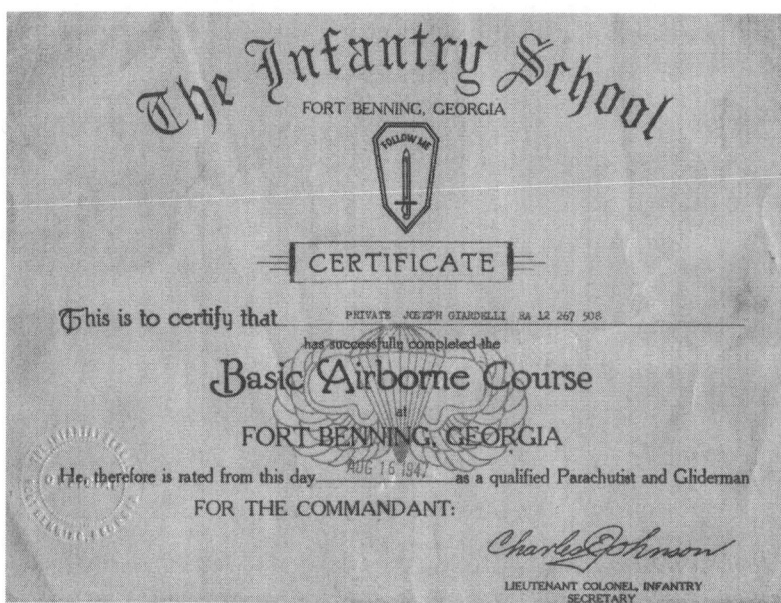

Private Giardello qualifies as a parachutist and gliderman, August 16, 1947.

Promotional illustration for Giardello/Webb fight, November 19, 1958. The caption read: "It'll be Right vs. Right at the Cow Palace tonight! Joey Giardello has one of the best right hands in the business...he broke Bobby Boyd's jaw with it!"

Giardello was cited in the U.S. House of Representatives for induction into the New Jersey Boxing Hall of Fame.

Giardello's bronzed championship gloves.

Joey Giardello Honors and Awards

2011 ~ Philadelphia dedicated statue of Giardello

2009 ~ Philadelphia Sports Hall of Fame

2001 ~ Pennsylvania Sports Hall of Fame

1999 ~ New Jersey Sports Writers Association Hall of Fame

1993 ~ International Boxing Hall of Fame

1990 ~ World Boxing Hall of Fame

1988 ~ Delaware Valley Italian-American Sports Hall of Fame

1987 ~ New Jersey Boxing Hall of Fame

1986 ~ New Jersey Chapter Italian-American Sports Hall of Fame

1979 ~ National Italian-America Sports Hall of Fame

1972 ~ Veteran Boxing Association, Ring 1, Pennsylvania Boxing Hall of Fame

1963 – 1965 ~ World Middleweight Boxing Champion

Giardello championship belt

JOEY GIARDELLO RING RECORD provided by John DiSanto, PHILLY BOXING HISTORY

JOEY GIARDELLO

Carmine Orlando Tilelli. Brooklyn. New York

Middleweight 07/16/1930 – 09/04/2008

101-25-7 / 33 KO / 1 NC

YEAR	DATE	OPPONENT	RESULT	SITE
1948	Oct. 2	Johnny Noel	KO2	Trenton
	Oct. 10	Jimmy Larkin	KO1	Atlantic City
	Nov. 7	Bobby Clark	W4	Wilkes-Barre
	Nov. 16	Jackie Cole*	KO1	Trenton
	Nov. 20	Johnny Brown	KO4	Reading
	Dec. 16	Johnny Madison	KO1	Atlantic City
	Dec. 30	Willie Wigfall	KO1	Philadelphia

1949

Feb. 24	Clyde Diggs	D6	Philadelphia
Mar. 15	Don Ennis	KO4	Reading
Apr. 7	Bill Montgomery	KO1	Philadelphia
Apr. 25	Ray Morris	W4	Wilkes-Barre
Apr. 28	Joe Aurillo	W6	Philadelphia
May 2	Emerson Charles	W4	Philadelphia
Jun. 6	Henry Vonsavage	KO2	Philadelphia
Jun. 20	Ray Haas	KO3	Philadelphia
Jul.13	Leroy Fleming	KO1	Washington. DC
Nov. 14	Mitchell Allen	W6	Philadelphia
Dec. 5	Jim Dockery	KO2	Philadelphia

1950

Jan. 5	Johnny Fry	W6	Philadelphia
Jan. 16	Joe DiMartino	L8	New Haven
Jan. 26	Johnny Bernardo	W8	Philadelphia
Feb. 9	Johnny Bernardo	W8	Philadelphia
Mar. 23	Armando Amanini	W8	Brooklyn
Mar. 27	Steve Sabatino	KO1	Philadelphia
Mar. 29	Johnny Brown	W6	Allentown
Apr. 20	Tommy Varsos	KO1	Brooklyn
May 4	Hurley Sanders	W8	Brooklyn
May 17	Carey Mace	KO'd 8	New York
Aug. 25	Al Berry	KO1	Scranton
Sep. 26	Ted DiGiammo	KO1	Wilkes-Barre
Oct. 16	Bruce Ubaldo	W8	Wilkes-Barre
Oct. 26	Harold Green	KO'd 6	Brooklyn
Nov. 27	Gene Roberts	D8	Philadelphia
Dec. 18	Leroy Allen	KO5	Philadelphia

1951

Jan. 6	Freddie Lott	W8	Brooklyn
Feb. 10	Jan Henry	W8	Philadelphia
Feb. 22	Hal Sampson	W8	Brooklyn
Feb. 24	Tony Wolfe	KO3	Philadelphia
Mar. 15	Roy Wouters	L8	Philadelphia
Mar. 29	Primo Cutler	W8	Philadelphia
Apr. 12	Roy Wouters	W8	Philadelphia
Apr. 30	Ernie Durando	W10	Scranton
May 25	Gus Rubicini	L8	New York
Aug. 13	Otis Graham	W8	Philadelphia
Aug. 27	Johnny Noel	W8	Philadelphia
Sep. 14	Tommy Bazzano	W6	New York
Oct. 8	Tony Amato	KO7	New York
Nov. 13	Rocky Castellani	L10	Scranton
Dec. 12	Bobby Dykes	L10	Miami Beach

1952

Jan. 9	Sal DiMartino	D10	Miami Beach
Mar. 28	Sammy Giuliani	D8	New York
May 5	Joe Miceli	D10	Scranton
Jun. 5	Roy Wouters	W6	Philadelphia
Jun. 23	Pierre Langlois	W10	Brooklyn
Aug. 4	Billy Graham	W10	Brooklyn
Sep. 15	Georgie Small	W10	Brooklyn
Oct. 13	Joey Giambra	W10	Brooklyn
Nov. 11	Joey Giambra	L10	Buffalo
Dec. 19	Billy Graham	W10	New York

1953

Feb. 2	Harold Green	W10	Brooklyn
Mar. 6	Billy Graham	L12	New York
Apr. 7	Gil Turner	W10	Philadelphia
May 30	Hurley Sanders	W10	Newark. NJ
Jun. 26	Ernie Durando	W10	New York
Sep. 29	Johnny Saxton	L10	Philadelphia
Oct. 26	Walter Cartier	W10	Brooklyn
Nov. 23	Tuzo Portuguez	W10	Brooklyn

1954

Jan. 8	Garth Panter	KO5	New York
Feb. 5	Walter Cartier	KO1	New York
Mar. 19	Willie Troy	KO7	New York
May 21	Pierre Langlois	L10	New York
Jun. 11	Bobby Jones	W10	New York
Jul. 7	Billy Kilgore	W10	Philadelphia
Sep. 24	Ralph Tiger Jones	W10	Philadelphia

1955

Jan. 25	Al Andrews	W10	Norfolk
Feb. 15	Andy Mayfield	KO8	Miami Beach
Mar. 1	Peter Mueller	KO2	Milwaukee

1956

Feb. 11	Tim Jones	KO10	Trenton
Mar. 10	Hurley Sanders	W10	Patterson
Mar. 27	Joe Shaw	W10	Philadelphia
May 7	Charlie Cotton	L10	New York
May 28	Charlie Cotton	L10	New York
Jul. 2	Tony Baldoni	KO1	New York
Jul. 26	Franz Szuzina	W10	Milwaukee

Aug. 28	James Kid Bussey	KO9	Miami Beach
Sep. 28	Bobby Boyd	KO5	Cleveland
Nov. 15	Charlie Cotton	W10	Milwaukee
Dec. 14	Charlie Cotton	W10	Cleveland

1957

Feb. 6	Randy Sandy	W10	Chicago
Mar. 27	Willie Vaughn	NC10	Kansas City
May 17	Rory Calhoun	W10	Cleveland
Jul. 2	Joe Gray	KO6	Detroit
Jul. 17	Chico Vejar	W10	Louisville
Sep. 27	Bobby Lane	KO7	Cleveland
Nov. 5	Wilfred Greaves	W10	Denver
Dec. 27	Ralph Tiger Jones	W10	Miami Beach

1958

Feb. 12	Franz Szuzina	W10	Philadelphia
May 5	Rory Calhoun	W10	San Francisco
Jun. 11	Franz Szuzina	W10	Wash., DC
Jun. 30	Joey Giambra	L10	San Francisco
Nov. 19	Spider Webb	KO'd 7	San Francisco

1959

Jan. 28	Ralph Tiger Jones	L10	Louisville
May 6	Holly Mims	W10	Wash., DC
Jun. 16	Del Flanagan	KO1	St. Paul
Aug. 11	Chico Vejar	W10	St. Paul
Sep. 30	Dick Tiger	L10	Chicago
Nov. 4	Dick Tiger	W10	Cleveland

1960

Apr. 20	Gene Fullmer	D15	Bozeman. MT
	For NBA 160 Title		
Sep. 27	Clarence Hinnant	KO3	Billings. MT
Oct. 11	Terry Downes	L10	London. ENG
Dec. 1	Peter Mueller	L10	Cologne. GER

1961

Mar. 6	Ralph Dupas	L10	New Orleans
May 15	Wilfred Greaves	KO9	Philadelphia
Jul. 10	Henry Hank	L10	Detroit
Sep. 12	Jesse Smith	W10	Philadelphia
Nov. 6	Jesse Smith	W10	Chicago
Dec. 12	Joe DeNucci	D10	Boston

1962

Jan. 30	Henry Hank	W10	Philadelphia
Jul. 9	Jimmy Beecham	W10	St. Paul
Aug. 6	George Benton	L10	Philadelphia
Nov. 12	Johnny Morris	W10	Baltimore

1963

Feb. 25	Wilfred Greaves	W10	Jacksonville
Mar. 25	Ernie Burford	W10	Philadelphia
Jun. 24	Ray Robinson	W10	Philadelphia
Dec. 7	Dick Tiger	W15	Atlantic City
	Won World 160 Title		

1964

Apr. 17	Rocky Rivero	W10	Cleveland
May 22	Rocky Rivero	W10	Cleveland
Dec. 14	Rubin Hurricane Carter	W15	Philadelphia
	World 160 Title Defense		

1965

Apr. 23	Gil Diaz	W10	Cherry Hill. NJ
Oct. 21	Dick Tiger	L15	New York
	Lost World 160 Title		

1966

Sep. 22	Cash White	W10	Reading
Dec. 5	Nate Collins	KO'd 8	San Francisco

1967

May 22	Jack Rodgers	L10	Pittsburgh
Nov. 6	Jack Rodgers	W10	Philadelphia

* This bout is sometimes omitted from Giardello's record (making it 100-25-7 / 32 KO / 1 NC)

About the Author

Charles Redner spent the majority of his career working in the advertising, television, and publishing worlds. He earned a BA in Psychology at Rutgers University, graduated from the Bessie V. Hicks School of Dramatic Arts and received a commission from the New Jersey State Military Academy.

Among his many career achievements, Charles produced and appeared on *Modern Living,* a live daytime television show in the Philadelphia market, produced the Philadelphia Phillies baseball pre-game TV show, and wrote and created hundreds of advertisements in print and broadcast media for many regional clients including Subaru and Ford. He is the past publisher of *Delaware Valley Business* magazine, Philadelphia, PA; *Broker Agent* magazine, Tucson, AZ, and *The Hummingbird Review*, a biannual literary journal.

Charles is a member of the Society of Southwestern Authors, and a past board member of the Philadelphia Public Relations Association, and Television & Radio Advertising Club of Philadelphia.

Originally from New Jersey, Charles and his wife, Judith, now live in Laguna Woods, California.

www.CharlesRedner.com

Acknowledgments

I wish to thank the entire Tilelli family for their cooperation and patience—with a special tribute to Joey Giardello's wife, Rosalie, without whom this story never could have been fully told. To their sons Joseph, Carman, Paul, and Steven; grandchildren Joseph, Michael, Gabriella, Carmine, Steven, and Sophia Rose: Walk proud. Your father/grandfather bequeaths you a monumental legacy. A special thanks to Joey's friend, Mike Santarpio. Without his vote of confidence, this story would not have escaped the tape recorder.

Gratitude to the Honorable Justice Anne Burke of the Illinois Supreme Court, for the generous gift of her time and for the lifetime commitment she has made to children with special needs. Thanks also to her administrative assistant, Lee Howard, for guiding me through the halls of justice. Recognition to executive director, Muncie Buckalew, and her staff at St. John of God School, Westville Grove, New Jersey. Appreciation extended to Cherry Hill Township Mayor Bernie Platt, the municipal workers and the entire police force. Your remembrances told with love and affection bring to life the happiest days of Carman Tilelli, those days he spent working beside you. I would be remiss if I didn't single out Carman's immediate superior during most of his employment at Cherry Hill Township, Gary Kanefsky.

Thanks to attorney George Brochetto, who provided details on *The Hurricane* movie lawsuit. Also to Joey's boxing community friends, Chico Vejar and Al Certo, who told stories about Giardello's generosity and that of the other fighters from the Golden Age of Boxing. A tip of the hat to Adeyinka Makinde for his book *Dick Tiger—The Life And Times of A Boxing Immortal,* a fine reportage on the man who gave Giardello the opportunity to fight for the middleweight championship title.

To John DiSanto, Philly Boxing History and the Philadelphia Veteran Boxing Association, Ring One, for their continued drive to bestow honor on the man and his accomplishments. Much thanks to Bernard Fernandez of the *Philadelphia Daily News,* for his shared memories of Giardello. A salute to Joe Rein, award-winning boxing writer who witnessed and provided the funniest pre-fight story retold here.

Major thanks to the many Down syndrome organizations, families, and children who welcomed me into their lives. To the planners and sponsors of the Los Angeles and Tucson Buddy Walks and the many families who freely shared their world, I salute you. To Tom Lambke and his son, Bryan, who told their Special Olympics stories, invited me into their home and allowed me to wear one of Bryan's gold medals, even if only for a few minutes.

No greater thanks than to the Scholnick family, Jack and his wife Marie, their son, Mickey, and daughter, Francine. If not for Jack's insistence, support and love, this project would never have made it beyond the talking stage.

For the authors who have inspired, editors who have guided, family and friends who have encouraged, I give thanks: Joseph Chiaravalotti, Gary DiGirolamo, Michael Gillespie, Judith Jordan, Jamie Kelly McCloskey, Tom Ong, Kaye Patchett, Robert Mansfield, Luis Urrea and my wife, Judith.

I extend a very, very special acknowledgment to my editor, Robert Yehling.

Printed in Great Britain
by Amazon.co.uk, Ltd.,
Marston Gate.